WHY TWO WORLDS?

BY

F. SIDNEY MAYER

AMS PRESS
NEW YORK

WHY TWO WORLDS?

THE RELATION OF PHYSICAL
TO SPIRITUAL REALITIES

BY

F. SIDNEY MAYER

The Pattern of a New Social Order

J. B. LIPPINCOTT COMPANY
PHILADELPHIA

Reprinted from the edition of 1934, Philadelphia

First AMS edition published in 1972

Manufactured in the United States of America

International Standard Book Number:0-404-08465-6

Library of Congress Catalog Card Number: 78-134425

AMS PRESS INC.
NEW YORK, N.Y. 10003

CONTENTS

CHAPTER I

THE MIND LOOKS INTO THE WORLD

I have a house inside of me:
A house that people never see;
It has a door through which none pass,
And windows, but they're not of glass.

But still I know what's really me
Lives in a house folks never see.

THE mind of man has many windows, and there is more than one way of looking at the world. Emerson, speaking of great men, says: "Shakespeare, Chaucer, Homer and Dante saw the splendor of meaning that plays over the visible world; they knew that a tree had another use than for bearing apples, and corn another than for meal, and the ball of the earth another than for tillage and roads; they knew that these things bear a second and finer harvest to the mind of man, being emblems of his thought, and conveying in all their processes and natural history a certain mute commentary on human life."

The human eye cannot see the microscopic particles of matter, nor note the universal motion and speed of the planet, but the seasons have their effect on nature, and on the mental states of individuals. There are two kinds of light, and each has its shadows; one light is physical, and the other mental. There are miracles of plant, animal and human birth, and these active phenomena are a perpetual observance. The plant and tree grow in size and beauty because they are chemical factories converting the compounds of sunlight, soil and moisture into orderly and visible forms. Nature has its peculiar influence on the human thought, and its rhythm of time and stress has its relationship with the mind of man. The mind can look up to the world, fascinated by the contour of its shell, or it can look down on the world and perceive the pulsations of the world's heart. One window presents the reality of matter, another window the reality of spirit.

> Two men look out through the same bars:
> One sees the mud, and one the stars.

A little child, absorbed in its play, fashions objects out of soft clay and creates for them a reality out of its own mental innocence. The growing youth shapes things out of wood, and in his adolescence he may draw the harmony of sound from dried catgut and wooden-bellied fiddle. The Indian searches wood and field for herb and pigment to heal his body and dye his fabrics. The real and the super-real are so closely interwoven that one hesitates to mark the dividing line. The arts and industries of the world are motivated by the undying force of man's will-power, yet, men dealing with material things live, get rich, and die, with their hearts and minds clinging to things which cannot speak, and cannot think, but yield submissively to the power of human minds.

There is another window of the mind through which one can see beyond the thing to the creative force which is distant, yet near, invisible yet impressionable, to a power which makes the visible object possible. In this vision the object is seen as a parable containing an undetected reality, an allegory which envelops a moral and religious truth. The scientist analyzes the tangible thing, the poet visualizes the force within the thing, and sets his idea to words and music because lyric symbolism has its roots imbedded in the finer emotions of common men. Epic and dramatic poetry, depending on strength and range, have consequences which are permanent in the nature of man. If we had no emotions beyond the fascination of material things, then no appeal, no matter how vivid and compelling, could ever attract them. The Hebrew poetry of the Old Testament has enduring values because the allegory and song parallel that which every man at some time sings in his own heart. Poetry is idealized experience, but it has its basis in human life and common affairs.

The science window and the mystic window present two aspects of the world; it is the same world of light and shadow, but the response depends on how one understands the light. The problem of the mind is the nature of light. The thought-feeling of the poet penetrates beyond the effect of the light to the source of light, and by means of its perceptive powers he weaves the nebulous and arcanic threads into the fiber of his verse and prose. In the gossamer texture he strives to transmit his vision until it glows for other eyes.

Is not the creation story of Genesis the symbol parable of all creation, the gradual becoming, the activity of form under the impulse of gyrating pure motion? Whatever becomes is the effect of prior cause; this applies the same to thought, idea, machine or animal.

Creation is a continuous process, a daily performance, which has its everlastingness; every object and particle is under the sway of its magic wand, submitting to the changing panorama of light and shadow, of death and resurrection. Under pressure myriads of petals form one drop of perfume, and the pleasures and agonies of a generation produce one historic epoch.

Every action and object has esthetic beauty for him who looks for beauty. Fortunately for us, not all look

through the same window; existence would become pro-
saic and monotonous if all experience were similar.
Ideas are contagious, thoughts are companionate, it
requires as many minds to produce a great image and
fix it as it does petals to distill one drop of enduring
fragrance. The mind of man is a hatchery in which
mental images breed, just as this world is the stuff
which gives creative force its enveloping forms.

Language is the symbol into which thought is
crystallized, and the crystals repay examination. Like
dry vegetable bulbs, when planted they will flower into
many forms of symmetrical beauty and radiant color.
Therefore we cannot destroy the symbols accumulated
through human experience during past ages. Egyptian,
Persian, Chinese and Mayan cultures produced symbols which have had many incarnations and their vitality is not exhausted.

Time is a limited, mechanical device which cannot
serve us in measuring thought or love. Time was not
the cause of the slowness with which man labored to
understand the physical universe; it lay rather in
mental incapacity, in the inability to conceive a great
phenomenon in the setting of its own reality. Creation
is large and continuous and it requires mental comprehension and application. There were ages when men
lived and loved, fought and died, firm in the belief that
this world was the center of the universe, and that its
flat surface blended into a fringe of cloud and water.
Today, we know that our solar system is a mere spot
of light in the Milky Way, and that our world is kin
to others in the endless galaxy. Our immediate physical dimension has shrunk, our dispositions and experiences are still with us, and the horizons of thought and
affection have expanded.

How the first seeds emanated, or how the original

framework of our architectural body assembled itself, no one knows. A molten mass could contain no germinal form on its surface after it cooled. Mineral substances in contact with degrees of air and moisture may have produced forms which gave vegetative activity a foothold, but the gap between symbiotic plants and animals is difficult to bridge. The physical can only evolve forms which yield to the animation of some force yet undiscovered. Man, as we know him, has a physical form which registers the moods of his affections; and this desire is controlled by an intelligence gained from experiences both outside and within himself. In this performance he stands alone among the animals; his instincts are animal, but his intuitions transcend his material boundaries and soar to heights which he himself cannot fathom. Certainly man could not have arrived as an individual until human reason dominated emotion and directed energy. On that day or in that era, man was in the becoming, and whatever form preceded this could not be classified as man.

The mystery of human evolution must be read in the child, for the vestigial germs have left their traces here, and not in the geologic deposits of rock and sand. Not the body of the infant, but the mentality of the infant must have been the state in which man first became conscious of himself and of the world. The evolution was more a development of emotion and intelligence than of bodily structure. The progress of civilization is measured in mental and emotional apprehension of consequences, in the use of experience in avoiding defeat and achieving success, rather than in change of bodily form. The understanding of things, both visible and invisible, is a victory of the mind and not of the muscle. In the human evolution we have progressed from the infant mentality to that of the child, perhaps we are now coming to the stage of youth, when human reason tackles the problem of life, searching for the meaning and purpose of existence; in this quest, youth may be devoid of mellowness and careless of traditional beliefs and formulas.

In the advance from primitive mentality—the level where sensuous knowledge is accepted as fact—there is a struggle to harmonize the acquired facts with the inner experience. The mind is not satisfied with its single-standard conclusions. Primitive people live in communities because individual consciousness has not been developed. The person does not feel adequate in and as of himself. Obedience is to the chief, the head of the tribe; all labor is for the benefit of the group, and the spirit of competition is unknown. In this condition every member of the group takes on himself the responsibility of defending the tribe. When warfare becomes active it is the united group defending itself from the aggressor, and the conflict is not won by open battle, but by strategy and deception of the senses.

When attention is centered on the task of finding nourishment, of yielding to sex instincts, and in accumulating reserves for old age, the higher demands of the spirit are starved and unsatisfied. The person who depended on wealth finds that he has yearnings which money cannot satisfy, for he has a spirit equipment which is undeveloped and untrained, and it cries aloud for expression. The battle of the soul has its tragic moments. The struggle for existence is transferred to a higher level where the discord and confusion are symptoms of the conflict which the soul is making for individual articulation. Every natural pursuit has its enemies; agriculture has its destroying insects, blights and droughts; industry has its depressions, labor troubles, and deficiency of capital; education, whether by schools, pulpit or studio, deplores its unappreciative audience; government has its internal and external foes and difficulties.

But the real enemies of man are not material forces; they are within the individual. Passion, prejudice, and the love of dominion are the destructive foes of civilization and of just and equitable social reconstruction. It is this inner ego which is at variance with sensuous facts. Every development has its birth in the environment of mystery; there are processes which cannot be comprehended. There are successive changes in our ideas of man, and of the universe, and very often these are so radical and revolutionary that they upset all former theories. It becomes easier now to understand the universe than to comprehend the undercurrent of the human motives and mind. For it is always the mind which looks out of its window on the world, and the mystery involved is that mind is greater than the universe. The world is a schoolroom for the mind. Its objects may be regarded as toys or they may be employed as means to a purposeful end.

Curiosity, courage, and purpose belong to the mind; they are not material creations. The man who labors all day in bondage with hands and tools will have his dreams at night. He lives in a dream-world which has no duplicate in nature. His dream creations are an escape from the bondage of matter; his dream-environment is often new, pleasing and enchanting, and in its pictures he is portrayed as the conquering hero. The individual becomes aware that his inner experience is not part of the community affairs, for he contemplates them alone. He can understand the struggle which Jacob had with the angel during the night hours; he knows the feeling of Moses while in the presence of the fiery bush; he has been in the land where Joseph

saw the obedient sheaves, the lean and fat cattle.
Knowledge of these mystic states he keeps to himself.

It is thus that the primitive mentality discovers that
man has a dual nature, an inside and an outside world
toward whose forces he responds. In the primitive
state these reactions are largely emotional, lacking the
intelligent control, for reason has not yet developed to
a stage of directive command. But in the assurance of
duality, his propitiatory sacrifices are offered to the
spirit deities. His worship of idols is an attempt to fix
in clay, stone, and wood a being beyond his physical
sight. In attaining the consciousness of duality he has
eaten of a fruit formerly unknown to him, and his eyes
have been opened to a recognition of his real self. He
enters into a new slavery, because the old ideas cannot
be readily swept aside and they suddenly take on a
form of bondage. New freedom always has its responsibilities and its particular conflicts. In his attempts
to meet the adversary with the defensive armor of his
original intelligence he suffers defeat. Only in obedience to the new intuitions does he find safety and satisfaction; acting contrary to them he feels the impact of
a stain on his new manhood. The struggle between the
things of the sense-world and the things of the spirit
is upon him. His fact-method has built high monu-
ments which ultimately dissolve and crush him. His
consciousness of a truth, the technique of which he is
in ignorance, engulfs him in a flood of false reasoning.
It is typical of the stage in which primitive man decks
himself with the feathers of eagles and the skins of
strong animals, in the belief that thus their power is
transmitted to him. Strong in this belief, he becomes
cannibal because of the conviction that the virtue of
the victim passes to the one who eats human flesh.

The savagery of man has always ruthlessly destroyed the gifts of nature and of God in its quest for something which it cannot find. It has not understood the nature of its own cravings, for meekness and humility always inherit the earth. Man left to his own inventions would eventually destroy himself and his world. His madness and insanity are part of his evolution, for they bring on exhaustion and a solitariness which revive hope. The prodigal comes to himself, recognizes the chasm between man and swine, and sees the dream-picture of a father's home. At the moment of his imminent destruction an upper window of his mind has miraculously opened. He becomes aware of an unsuspected faculty, and recognizes that something within himself has saved him. As a result of the fierce struggle for knowledge he has gained a new foothold; everything his foot can tread upon is his, and his horizon reveals a new world. The rainbow of promise has built an arch across his darkest clouds, but yet, at the ends, it does not touch the ground.

> To trace love's faint beginnings in mankind,
> To know even hate is but a mask of love's,
> To see a good in evil, and a hope
> In ill-success; to sympathize, be proud
> Of their half-reasons, faint aspirings, dim
> Struggles for truth, their poorest fallacies,
> Their prejudice and fears and cares and doubts;
> All with a touch of nobleness, despite
> Their error, upward trending although weak,
> Like plants in mines which never saw the sun,
> But dream of him, and guess where he may be,
> And do their best to climb and get to him.

The upward trend is a primary characteristic of human nature, and it is quite evident that new things do come into the world through the minds of men. There has been a gradual development of the arts and sciences during the past centuries because some men have done serious thinking. The culture, modes, customs of the generation, attitudes toward things, and the use of natural resources, continually improve under the discoveries and inventions of men. When new processes and ideas are proven and accepted, the antiquated methods, credulities and superstitions are discarded and forgotten.

When we examine a plant, a rock or lump of clay, or an animal, our thought should be—What did Life plan as its ultimate use when this was formed? If we could lift its covering, understand its structure and operation, we would hear a silent voice speaking every moment to our ingenuity and skill, begging us to co-operate with life in utilizing it for our greater service in helping other men. Nature in its manifold forms is full of little windows through which we are invited to share in the future glory and power which creative Life is suggesting.

> The world unfolds its petals like a rose
>   A diamond flower of perfectness and joy;
> Its golden heart in morn's effulgence glows,
>   No more shall loathly worms its fruit destroy.
> 'Tis tearful April for it now; the streams
>   Run turbid with the melted snows of wrong.

Go back but a short space of time and note that the chemical action and formation of plants were unnoticed previous to the seventeenth century. Not until the latter part of the same century were the circulation and nature of the blood seriously studied. Prior to 1860 nature was supposed to consist of only five elements of matter. The telephone, auto, radio, airplane, X-ray, and radium are in common use to-day, but the world went ignorantly along without them up to fifty years ago. During the preceding centuries men were struggling with the elemental facts, developing vocabularies, shaping domestic utensils and ornaments, and loading the backs of obedient beasts with their heavy burdens.

Under the whip of adversity the mind of man rebelled and reached out to the unknown, and when the answering assurance came it brought with it a light to point the upward path. Men considered it accidental when they stumbled onto the secret working of some hitherto unnoticed law of nature, or some composition of an unknown element; this exclamation of surprise inspired other men to experiment, to test the propositions and postulates, and thus new things were created. Some scientists accept the doctrine of independent evolution, which, when reduced to the singular, means that when a new idea comes to some individual of inventive mind, there are persons in other parts of the world who are independently making the same discovery. As an example, Mayan civilization and architecture may be very much like that of Egypt or Persia, but each developed independent of and unknown to the other. Others contend for the diffusion theory which claims that man is imitative; that is, any given trait of culture is invented only once, and it is multiplied through the world by imitation. Neither theory satisfies the reason.

Perhaps the deeper truth is—that new ideas are pressing through to this earth from the spiritual world, and wherever a mind is attuned to the infinite it registers the impressions and shapes them into an ultimate form of service. No human mind is operating alone in isolated outposts, and the flights of intelligence are combing the outer realms in search of something which can be brought down to earth. As in the arts and sciences, so also in the field of religion there is a new interpretation of the scriptures, a knowledge that experience is important in the development of character, and a finer recognition of the value of human relations. These ethical and spiritual ideas, born within the necessity of the times, are revelations which adjust the man to his world.

The growth of religious knowledge has been cumulative. The literature of the Bible is the product of twenty centuries, some of its parts written by men distant in time, but through it all is the consistent unfolding of the divine mind. Its language is largely symbol, allegory and parable, because spirit has no words of its own, and therefore uses the signs that man can understand. In the first Eden story it is indicated that the MAN would come, and down through the centuries the vision became more clear as prophets grasped the significance of the divine incarnation. These men of old had the ability to see farther, to hear distant music, and to translate their vision and sensations into prophetic words. Wherever we turn, it is from outside this material world that men get their inspiration, their hope and realizations. In ancient and modern Chinese philosophy a mystic trilogy is recognized; man conforms to the laws of heaven, and heaven harmonizes with earth.

When the masses are slumbering in the security of unrelated beliefs and accepted philosophies, the stage is set for a new world by those who see beyond the present and prepare the means by which it will be ushered in. These persons have the ability to pierce the outward and superficial surface of things to an understanding of their inner realities of goodness, truth and beauty. It was the psalmist of the Syrian plains, who lay on his back at night while his sheep were huddled close, who sang:—"The heavens declare the glory of God; and the firmament sheweth his handiwork."

Man is improved and developed by close grips with the necessities of nature, and out of this furnace of conflict comes the pure gold of his refined character.

We are all blind until we see
That in the common plan
Nothing is worth the making
If it does not make the man.

Why build these temples glorious
If man unbuilded goes?
We build a world in vain
Unless the builder also grows.

CHAPTER II

WHAT IS LIFE?

O Life! that mystery that no man knows,
And all men ask: the Arab from his sands,
The Caesar's self, lifting imperial hands,
And the lone dweller where the lotus blows.

O'er trackless tropics, and o'er silent snows,
She dumbly broods, that sphinx of all the lands;
And if she answers, no man understands,
And no cry breaks the blank of her repose.

THERE is a challenge in the doctrine of evolution that
demands a revised interpretation of the animating
power which is commonly called, Life. In every literature, Life lacks definition; the object which Life sets
into action is mistaken and confused with the principle
of Life. What Life is in itself is unknown. We see the
variety of forms which give it expression, and recognize the manifold effects which it produces, but Life
itself is a principle or power which escapes the physical
barriers of analysis. Our languages are deficient in a
vocabulary by which to define and express it.

Bishop Charles Fiske, writing recently in *The Atlantic Monthly*, quoted an unnamed author who wrote,
"If there is any living man who can say, in the face
of the living world around him, that he does not believe in the irresistible, enabling, marvelous certainty
of Life, he can be left to his own devices. It does not
in the least matter that Life is inexplicable and incom-
prehensible. The fact is that, the more a man is alive,
the more he knows that he's alive. The more he thinks

and reads, the more he is struck by the achievements of Life on earth. Life *everlasting* seems more difficult, but the adjective is one upon which science, however reluctantly, is being more and more desperately driven."

Any observer can recognize that there is a continual series of births, growths, developments and changes, going forward in every segment of the world known to man. This has always been true, and the power producing these changes has never consulted or waited on man for advice or assistance. This constant movement is not limited to things material, but forces its process into every feeling and thought, every national and individual experience. Life itself has powers, forces and qualities, exceeding in extent and creativeness anything which is inherent in the things which it animates. Life is not a distant power manipulating the universe from the outside. Life works in and through all things, material, ethical and spiritual. If "the universe is but one vast symbol," as Carlyle affirms, then we must carefully read the symbols and learn what they teach us of the character of Life. That the symbols can be arranged in a series of order, and that the universe both great and small observes the same law of order, and that man himself can be developed in definite order, assists us in understanding that Life is inherently order. Order then is one of Life's qualities and characteristics.

Birth, progress and decay seem to have an ultimate purpose, and judged by the consequences, we are compelled to admit that Life has purpose. We cannot hastily conclude that Life has mind, and yet it is difficult to escape that conviction, for we know that order and purpose are impossible among human beings without the exercise of mental faculties. There may be meas-

ures and degrees inherent in Life which are unknown
to us, because its quality, its possibilities, and its ultimate purpose are largely veiled and not yet evident.
We cannot assume with sophisticated assurance that
a thing is true as stated, for there are many challenges
in the study of Life. Philosophers have simply accepted
Life because they cannot deny it, but they have given
us no conclusive definition. Its qualities and dimensions
escape the mathematical calculations of Euclid, the
philosophy of Plato, and the theologic speculations
of Aquinas. To define Life as God merely begs the
question and delays the inquiry. If births have purpose
then the thing born achieves something, and the goal
has been anticipated in the Life which inspired the
birth. The original conception, the thing born and developed, and the goal achieved, are three separate and
distinct manifestations, each of different quality and
degree. The mind that visualizes an idea, the machine
constructed in conformity with the idea, and the use
which the machine performs, are not alike in substance;
they have combined for a purpose, but each retains its
individuality. Life cannot act by itself for ultimate
purpose unless it finds an instrumental form through
which it can achieve its end. The mechanism into which
Life flows will largely determine the perfection or
effectiveness of the purpose produced; a defective
mechanism may even defeat the original purpose. In
the birth of an individual, Life may have high purposes in view, but Life is at the mercy of the man's
mentality and his own will to do. Diseased plants cannot produce perfect fruit, mixed gases may be destructive, metals in certain environments kill men, disorderly
thoughts produce disease, salty literature breeds immorality. If Life has granted power to the mechanism
which it cannot control, then Life can be defeated.

However, a knowledge of biology and of symbiosis will readily teach us that defective forms cannot breed and that they destroy themselves, because Life cannot act constructively through them.

The scientists and the mystics view Life from different vantage points; they are often wrong in their denials, but right in their affirmations. The world thought has not advanced sufficiently from its several beginnings to the point where their paths converge. If man is the consummation, the most perfect product of creation, then a knowledge of what man really is would help in defining the Life which produced him. But, how many would agree on any conceivable definition of man? Some contend that he has eternal possibilities which transcend the boundaries of this world; others would claim that he is an object of insignificant stature, incapable of understanding the laws of his own universe, and untrained in the control of the elements which are carrying him to destinations which he cannot avoid. Can these two ideas be reconciled, can thought which is honestly searching for truth always be mistaken, and is it never right? Youth, in its haste, may believe that all things are settled, but maturity is disillusioned and knows that problems have no final solution. Every age has its own problems and must find its own solutions; its defeats are confined to the stage of its own theater, but its victories are passed on to succeeding generations.

Is man the result of accident? Could evolution have given us a creature not in the calculations of Life? The fact that few planets known to our telescopic eyes are capable of sustaining human beings would be a strong argument for this conclusion, but the universe is so vast that there may easily be in it countless earths with conditions favorable to human habitation. On those planets the human mechanism may differ from ours, and may be adjusted to the environment. Judging Life by its own performance, it seems improbable that man was not within its calculations and purpose. A. R. Wallace says, "The Darwinian theory, even when carried to its extreme logical conclusions, not only does not oppose, but lends a decided support to, a belief in the spiritual nature of man. It shows us how man's body may have been developed from that of a lower animal form under the law of natural selection; but it also teaches us that we possess intellectual and moral faculties which could not have been so developed, but must have had another origin; and for this origin we can only find an adequate cause in the unseen universe of spirit." Man's sensuous mechanism registers the impact of his environment; his physical and mental organisms conform to everything we know of nature, matter, and spirit. His mind reaches out to realms unknown to nature, and within himself he seems to stand actually between two worlds, neither one of which he fully comprehends. Wordsworth saw this fitness of the external world as the mirror and emblem of man's spiritual and moral consciousness:

> How exquisitely the individual Mind
> (And the progressive power, perhaps no less
>   Of the whole species) to the external World
> Is fitted :—and how exquisitely, too—
> The external World is fitted to the Mind.

Taking a long-range view, man has potential possibilities the extent of which has not entered the fondest dreams. It is upon the deeds and inspiration of the past that he always rebuilds the hope of the future. If this fact has any implications, it means that man is not confined to his single generation, but has elements of futurity which involve eternity. By penetrating the finer thought of the race, in literature, science and adventure, and striving for the utmost capacity of his mental reach, he is continually inspired to renewed effort. He has the sustaining intellect and stimulating emotion which quicken his desire to drink deeply of the beauty of thought, and the glory of action. The sustained youth of man is one of the marvelous works of Life; Stopford Brooke has caught the sentiment which gives to man the quiet strength that carries him as a passport through the world:

> So simple is the earth we tread,
>   So quick with love and life her frame,
> Ten thousand years have dawned and fled,
>   And still her magic is the same.
>
> So simple is the heart of man,
>   So ready for new hope and joy:
> Ten thousand years since it began
>   Have left it younger than a boy.

Man at his best is ever seeking the beauty of order, in himself, in his family, and in government. He would not persist in this effort if he were not aware that in himself are the possibilities of a corresponding order. The mechanics of his physical structure are organized, they function for a common welfare; the mind can be trained to a compliance with order and thus organize itself for useful ends. It is not a matter of intellectual assent or dissent, for man is being urged by a prior impulse through groping thought and individual effort toward a perfection which in its finality resides in Life itself. Any one might easily doubt this, especially when observing the daily pursuits and pleasures of average people, but back of their small talk and petty affairs, consciousness of greater things may be in the making.

Sir Isaac Newton is regarded as a serious thinker, but he confessed that, "I do not know what I may appear to the world; but to myself I seem to have been only like a boy playing on the seashore, and diverting myself in now and then finding a smoother pebble or a prettier shell than ordinary, whilst the great ocean of truth lay all undiscovered before me."

Regardless of the retrogressions, the race is moving to higher and untried levels, to more complete understandings of its place in the march of time. It is forging its own link in the chain which binds it to the past and the future, to this world and a world yet to come. The spark within him, which we call Life, pervades and permeates every cell of his body and every impulse of his mind. If man was ever capable of being shocked into a state of hopelessness by the failure of the race there have been more than enough of defeats, barriers and catastrophes to have discouraged and disheartened him centuries ago. The facility with which man has overcome all obstructions is due to the fact that he has a double set of experiences; the experience acquired from his contact with the objective world, and the experience which comes to him through consciousness of Life energies. The sensuous experience can be verified by the usual scientific methods; the inner spirit experience, which is individual, can be verified by the progressive idealism of the race as a whole, and is found in the spiritual springs which have carried it forward. The hope, confidence, and consciousness of Life's eternal purposes, which have carried the individual onward, are the same hope, confidence and consciousness that have buoyed up the race during periods of war, depression, scourge and famine. In every darkest hour these qualities have asserted themselves, they are the mainstay of the single pioneer, and of the nation and race. It is Life itself which will not be defeated, and as man is motivated by the Life he shares its convictions and hopes. Man is advanced by the velocity of Life to ends which serve a greater purpose than he can now understand.

It is man alone who can put Life to a practical test. Theories are constantly given birth in the ovum of his pregnant hope, and he is continually exposing these emotional and mental children to his own sense of experience, and observing their actual demonstration. He is obedient to what he understands at the moment, for only by the results obtained can it prove its right to exist. Man is often compelled to do something which to him seems unavailing, and is surprised that in doing it he has developed a new and unused capacity which can be trained for future service. Not the thing he does, or its product, but the effort within the act has been a revelation. Doing the wrong and unwise act often has future possibilities. The mistakes of Persia and the folly of Egypt added brilliance to the genius of Greece and Rome. Grasses attempt to grow on soil that cannot support them, but each succeeding crop adds its fertility to the soil for the welfare of oncoming crops and vegetation. Martha's complaint to Jesus brought out the lesson of two kinds of service, and the inconstancy of the Samaritan woman was instrumental in elucidating the fact that true worship is not in temples, but in individual obedience. Every rejection improves the standard of selection, and out of revolution comes the new and better order. Man never accomplishes everything in a single effort. As the Caucasian mountaineers say, "You cannot pick up six watermelons at one time with one hand." Judged wholly by outward appearances men seem to be acting, as Shaliapin, the Russian, has said, "like a performance

of grand opera by a troupe which is perfectly competent, but which has no conductor, and never had a re-
hearsal." The conductor is the unseen Life, and certainly all precedents do not point to the probability of
a final period of anemic-discord.

When man observes the world he lives in he sees
purpose written across its bosom, and the finger-prints
of Life can be read where they have left indelible marks.
John Ruskin, in *Stones of Venice*, expresses the thought
that, "It is not an accidental necessity for the convey-
ance of truth by pictures, instead of words, which led
to the universal adoption of symbolism wherever art
was on the advance, God would have us understand all
things amidst which we live; there is a deeper meaning
within them than eye hath seen or ear heard, and that
the whole visible creation is a mere perishable symbol
of things eternal and true." Progress in organization,
material and mental, is the unvarying urge of man,
because order and organization are Life working out
its own perfection in the world through man. The
world's greatest literature, the Bible, begins with the
story of a garden, in which is both good and evil, it
ends with the vision of a holy city, perfectly organized
and coördinated. Its gates open to all points of the
compass, so that every type of mind may enter that
can qualify for its unselfish service. Refusal to read the
signs or to heed the sequence of events seems like
bondage to an inexcusable ignorance, and is not keeping step with the spirit of man. In the *Kasidah* of Haji
Abdu El-Yezdi we have these lines:

> With ignorance wage eternal war;
>   To know thyself forever strain,
> Thine ignorance of thine ignorance
>   Is thy fiercest foe, thy deadliest bane;

That blunts thy sense, and dulls thy taste;
    That deafs thine ears, and blinds thine eyes;
  Creates the thing that never was;
    The thing that ever is defies.

For evidence that Life needs man in completing its purposes we have only to observe the daily pursuits and occupations of civilization. Mankind has laboriously built upward from the agricultural pursuits to the era of the industrial machine age; it began writing its thought on rocks, clay and skins, employing characters pictured by birds and animals, and to-day it writes by machine and conveys ideas on invisible waves. The forms which Life created have never been wholly completed; they are largely in bulk and unseparated, purposely so left that man by ingenuity of invention may finish them in his own day for his enjoyment and sustenance.

The farmer cultivates the soil and plants the seed, then Life vitalizes the seed, producing blade, stalk and grain, and waits on man to harvest the crop, grind the kernel and bake the bread. The partnership of Life and man educates the worker and fulfills the eternal purpose of Life. Minerals lie imbedded in rock and mud, inviting the skill of man to fulfill their destiny; he draws them to the surface, and their refined values are shaped by the arts and crafts into utensils and ornaments which serve the needs of the human family. Man has not only dug into the earth, but he has reached out into invisible space and commanded the gases and atoms which lay there untouched for millions of years waiting for educated man to employ them in useful service. These well-known facts of common experience should not lead us to speak lightly of the future. There may be other elements in the storehouse of Life which will challenge coming generations, and it is safe to predict that Life has provided material for them in anticipation of a human knowledge which far excels any that is known to us. The dark ages are always behind us, and we are laggard in keeping up with the tempo of Life.

The march of history indicates that man should train himself in the art of observing, comprehending and meditating before he can master the skill of production on a grand scale. His inventive faculties are constantly appealed to, and one conquest makes more certain the success of the next venture. New inventions begin in simple and individual ideas, like scattered seeds which can combine to evolve new forms. One man sees an apple falling, another observes the steam that lifts the lid of a tea-kettle, then some one flies a kite with a copper wire and experiments with a door-key, while another gets a spark from exploding gas. Combine these ideas and you have the modern methods of transportation which conquer continents, lift man into space, and carry messages across continents. In the scheme of Life accidents have purpose—Gutenberg drops something, and we have the printing press; Daguerre stains his fingers with salts of silver, and we have photography; Edison observes a strange blue flame that interferes with his work, and we have the X-ray. Mystery and miracle are words that connote the unknown; they invite credulity until they are conquered.

The inward urge which drives man onward toward action needs a far more lucid explanation before we can understand the meaning of Life. Why is it that, when he is not at play, man is constantly devising the improvement of the things which he already has? We cannot dismiss the question by saying that he seeks happiness, for he would be far more content in simple

128 M452w
C. 1

surroundings, more peaceful in quiet meditation on sublimer subjects. Every invention adds to the comfort of the world, but it also increases the burden of responsibility. Modern machines have lifted the load from the muscles, and provided a leisure which cannot find enjoyment, and a wealth which is not wisely spent, a relief in which there is no contentment. Mark Hopkins, the educator, said, "Man has wants deeper than can be supplied by wealth or nature or domestic affections. His great relations are to his God and to eternity." Elizabeth Browning writes:

> With stammering lips and unsufficient sound
>   I strive and struggle to deliver right
> The music of my nature, day and night,
>   With dream and thought and feeling interwoven,
> And only answering all the senses round,
>   With octaves of a mystic depth and height,
> Which steps out grandly to the infinite,
>   From the dark edges of the sensual ground.

Why were men born to come this way regardless of its pain, and never hands could hold them back, nor cities lull with gain? It seems that we must experience all the thrills of Life—fecund, passionate, palpitating Life. A painting is an image of the lights and shadows of nature; a book is just the biography of personal experience; music is an imitation of the fall of waters, the wind sighing in the trees, the birds singing in the branches, and the hum of bees on the clover. We find our inspiration in these works of human art because Life crowds us on to its own finer destinies. James Russell Lowell writes: "No man is born into the world whose work is not born with him. There is always work, and tools to work withal, for those who will; and blessed are the horny hands of toil." Laboulaye thinks of man's search for truth, and says, "Truth is like a pearl: he alone possesses it who has plunged into the depths of Life and torn his hands on the rocks of Time."

> Slowly the Bible of the race is writ,
> Not on paper leaves or blocks of stone,
> Each age, each kindred adds a verse to it,
> Texts of hope or joy, or a moan.

In Cato we read, " 'Tis the divinity that stirs within us; 'tis heaven itself that points out an hereafter, and intimates eternity to man." Life cannot be created, everything is under its dominating sway; it seeks expression through every organized form that can be employed in its service. Nothing can be animated except Life enter in, and all is dead and non-existent which does not yield to Life. Religion personifies it and calls it God. The beauty of religion and the strength of its persistence are in this, the developed faith and confidence, and the desire to yield to its order always encourages and invites more of Life. Science simply admits that there is Life; there is no attempt to define it, for its qualities are unknown.

Man has two sides of contact: his emotional and mental self makes its contacts with the invisible entity called Life; through the sensitive physical body, man contacts with the objects of the material world, and performs his allotted tasks by virtue of the power which Life has given to him. The effect of his labor serves a purpose in which many may share. This service may be wholly mental as in literature, drama, music, science, and the higher arts; it may be physical, providing the infinite human requirements of food, shelter, transportation, and domestic necessities. But, back of all this machinery, it is Life which is seeking expression, and what we see and do are merely the tools at

work. A factory crowded with machines is simply dead
matter, when the switch is connected with the power
house the electric fluid finds a path and the shop hums
with speed and the output of the factory will supply
the needs of thousands of persons. The electric current
illustrates the force of Life; the machines correspond
to men, and the product is the accomplished end which
Life had in view. The three have been brought into
orderly relationship for a specific purpose. Illustrations
of this principle abound on every hand, and the process
and effect are always certain.

Life animates a universe of matter; the effect supplies the human mind with material for its development and adjustment. The world is the training ground
for the human faculties: it provides the images which
are woven into ideas and thoughts, and the relation
of objects and qualities that cluster around emotions.
Life, man, and the universe are interdependent: Life
is pure motion; matter is mechanical motion, and effect
is influential motion.

Life has been lavish in her expenditures to the end
that man may be educated; she is creating personality
out of the structure of nature and the paradoxical flow
of external world substance. If we concede that man
is being educated at so great an expense, then the
question arises, Why the effort, and for what end?

> We live in deeds, not years: in thoughts, not breaths,
> In feelings, not in figures on a dial.
> We should count time by heart throbs. He most lives
> Who thinks most, fells the noblest, acts the best.
> Yet truth and falsehood meet in seeming like
> The falling leaf and shadow on the pool's face.
> Men might be better if we better deemed
> Of them. The worst way to improve the world

Is to condemn it. Men may overget
Delusion, not despair.

Can we conclude that Life has in mind an ordered
purpose and is fully aware of the consequences; and
that man is an instrument inspired by Life to work out
its plans; and that the final result expresses the useful
service which Life has foreseen? If so, we have the
purpose, the mechanism through which it works, and
the finished product. Man is man because he has an
intelligence which can control emotional conduct and
direct it in definite channels to a conceived goal. If
Life has the power to inspire understanding and emotion, can we attribute these two qualities to Life? If
Life has intelligence, it must be perfect wisdom, and if
it has emotion, it must be infinite and unbounding love.
Disraeli was certainly a competent judge of human
nature; he has said, "To think, and to feel, constitute
two grand divisions of men of genius—the men of reasoning and the men of imagination." It is understanding and affection which enable men to plan, to execute
their desires, and to achieve their goals. The entire
realm of human affairs, past, present and future, comes
within that category. The process which man uses is
the principle on which Life acts. Man is very closely
kin to Life, and perhaps the real character of Life can
be dimly read in the feeble efforts of man.

Man differs from the forms beneath him in the scale
of creation. There is no consciousness of activity in
minerals and the lower animal forms. Vegetation processes are mechanical; each leaf is a chemical factory
limited by its own structure. The organized government of bees and termites is a marvel to man, but its
direction is not in the mentality of its inhabitants or
leaders. The egg of the queen bee can germinate as
male or female, but the conscious purpose lies in the

mind of Life and not that of the bee. Life has many
points of resistance beyond which it cannot act, but
this resistance produces a shell, and the shell of dead
matter forms finally a structure into which Life can
move and deposit its forces. The remains of myriads
of crustacea furnish material for chalk-beds and moun-
tains, and the material wisely distributed by man enriches the soil. Successful governments have been built
on prejudices and hatreds, and under the impress of
man's genius have gone on to a glory which disowned
its heritages. Religions have flourished on ground
where doubt and despair were strewn. The lily and
rose ravage the eye with gorgeous color and spread a
perfume over foundations which were dung and ashes.

It is by man alone that the forces of Life can be
understood; he is conscious of the deep wounds of
pain, and the heavenly delights which love have to
offer, and from this experience he is aware that Life
can feel the bitterness of its own rejection, and also
glory in its fulfilments. Love is the supreme emotion
which Life bestows upon man, and therefore its abuse
is the most deadly. No blade was ever sharpened that
can cut deeper than hatred, for hatred is the perverted
use of love. Hatred has a deformed brood of offspring,
animosity, aversion, malice, spite, revenge, and the
others which are disorderly manifestations of emotional
perversions.

The individual who uses Life according to her own
formula cultivates an inner sense of values; he develops
a conscience which is aware that Life suffers most in
her rejections. Life could not be aware of the range
and power of love unless Life itself is Love, nor would
it grant so powerful a weapon to man unless within
its own experience it understood the consequences.
Even with man's limited intelligence he can verify the

quality of love, its joy and pain, in its results. Men
have engaged themselves with the shells of insipid
things, and they have so often loved darkness more
than light that it is surprising with what extreme pa-
tience Life has continued in her task. Man accepts the
commonest because he is not accustomed to the enjoy-
ments of the excellent. Only by means of intelligence
can we judge the matters of every day by their eternal
values; the paraphernalia of reality has its moments
when we can recognize infinity through the veil of its
covering. It is the intelligent man who knows more
than one crisis, for he dies many times, and experiences
many resurrections. Life seems to select those fitted
for great service, and the pity is that they are so few
in a given population. Truth pays highly for a footing
in the world. Men who force open the gates of knowledge, and leave them open for others to pass through,
are called on to face prejudice and unbelief, for theirs
is not an adventure of gain and personal glory. Emerson has remarked that "the chambers of the great are
jails." The world places wreaths only on the departed;
it never recognizes its Dantes, Galileos, Newtons, Far-
adays, Darwins, and Listers until their fruits have
appeased a common taste. The dirge of this complaint
has been registered many times, but it gives some idea
of the struggle for recognition which Life is perpetually making in its battle for expression.

The span of man's existence, if limited to his years,
and the fact that he is ushered into the world with no
knowledge of the stupendous forces to which he can
respond, may excite no surprise when we consider the
latitude of his ineffectiveness. Our desires are infinite,
but their free and untrammeled gratification is
thwarted on all sides by insurmountable obstacles;
there are conflicts with the views of others, and ex-

perience is slow in forming correct judgments. Our
tutored knowledge begins by sharing the views of those
who have gone before, and if these are illogical and
cannot stand the test of time, their unlearning is difficult and taxes our resources.

Intelligence is developed slowly, but love is the free
gift of Life; therefore it is the task of intelligence to
control love, but love in the beginning is the mother
of intelligence. We can love wisely only when we
reason correctly. Our mind is so constructed that
thoughts and ideas can rise to heights where reason
cannot follow, and then fall to earth because they have
no secure foundations. In the poet's vision:

> Man can condense the sky into a glance,
> The wind within a sigh,
> The forest graveness in his countenance,
> The ocean in his cry.
> Man can combine the creatures in his deeds,
> The weather in his will,
> The universe of hope and growth, in seeds,
> And lie at last as still.

Nature is the schoolmaster, for Life has provided
the objective world so that man may acquire intelligence. If, in the course of events, man must learn to
know, then Life itself has intelligence that is perfect
wisdom, and Life shares its experience with him. There
is that mysterious need of a judgment on Life, of
which the most detached intellect cannot apparently
rid itself.

If the range of man's experimentation is conditioned
wholly by time and space, and if in all places and
periods the fundamental qualities of human nature
have been the same, then man will always, as in the
past, ponder the meaning and question of Life. While
a plausible definition of Life cannot be stated in words

and creeds, for it cannot so be bound, yet it has ways of repeating its own story into the ears and eyes of those who correctly observe and virtuously feel her pulsations.

> How many times the tale of spring
>   Is told to men!
> A truth each year that ev'rything
>   Must tell again.
> In winter men forget the sod,
>   The summer gone:
> The rediscovery of God
>   Must still go on.
> The truth forever must be shown,
>   If new or not;
> For there is nothing much unknown,
>   But much forgot.

The biologic sciences deal with the distinctive phenomena presented by living organisms, from microbes to mammals, and their activities. A living organism maintains its specific structure and activities throughout all changes. The stability of forms is maintained in the organism through an inner activity, and not mere passive resistance to changes in the environment. Life is a dynamic equilibrium which tends to maintain itself. An organism adapts itself to its environment, and replies to its changes. Should it be injured, the healing process sets in, and the process of reproduction starts in the organism itself. The organism and the environment are inextricably intertwined. There is a specific inner direction in organisms which grow, repair, reproduce themselves, and mold the outer circumstances into their own patterns. What we know of matter does not help us to understand the coördinated maintenance of Life, for Life is a different order of fact.

It is a human experience that the more one understands and loves, to that degree does he realize the fullness of Life in himself. Knowledge and experience are individual, and it is by means of these that Life confides her secret. Life's book of deeds is written in the objects of nature, and these are her symbols, but her esoteric teaching is revealed to those who love her, and employ her gifts to realize her desires.

You ask for a message. 'Tis this:
The only true knowledge is his
  Who sees by the inward light
The only reality is
  That which is hid from sight.

The work your hand findeth to do
Is the honor given to you
  All earthly honors above:
No hope is too good to be true:
  And nothing is greater than Love.

CHAPTER III

THE MIND AS SPIRIT

The pure, the beautiful, the bright,
　That stirred out hearts in youth,
The impulse to a wordless prayer,
　The dreams of love and truth,
The longings after something lost,
　The spirit's yearning cry,
The strivings after better hopes,
　These things can never die.

ANY person who has made a practice of keeping a diary in his youth will recognize that the events and experiences there recorded were accompanied by such opinions as frequently constitute the overflow of the active and excited mind of a student. However, these thoughts, when viewed in the perspective of years, do indicate a line of progress in unanticipated directions. These experiences are comparable to a rudderless bark wholly at the mercy of the moods of the sea, the havens and ports to which they finally come seem to have been reached by a providential guidance. While in the throes of significant events we often form conclusions hastily, and learn to understand their import later. By some intuitive sense we identify ourselves with their moods at the moment, and with the realities they open to our contemplation. In nature there is no wrong, everything is properly placed, the swamp and the worm, as well as the grass and the bird—all is there for itself. Only because we think that these things have a relation to us do they appear justifiable or condemnatory.

It is well to begin in youth to make notes of everything which is of interest above the ordinary. There is so much in human existence that is drab and sordid, and it is therefore well to decorate the blank walls of the mind with those things which are cheerful, charming and wholesome. There are blossoming vines and climbing roses to be planted at the threshold of the imagination; literary and poetic flowers to make the thought fragrant and inspiring; and rare word-pictures to fascinate and stimulate the emotions.

It is true that no one can succeed unless he works things out for himself, and submits to the discipline which the events impose upon him. There are many fine impressions which come to us at the formative period of youth, and these become part of our experience, and their lusterful pigments often color our later thinking. Everything that comes to us is attracted by an affection within ourselves, and thus the potential and primary causes are in the individual, and in working out they select those facts which satisfy their tastes. Training in self-criticism and confidence can be developed to a degree where they become vital and interesting, and they guard us from the external arts of flattery and internal depreciations, which often culminate in defeat. In all forms of experience there are definable laws of averages. Individuals see the effects of Life in different aspects. Some employ the fruits of experience solely for utilitarian ends; others, of an esthetic nature, accept experience as an end in itself, and this becomes an art.

Occasionally volcanic eruptions take place in the social world as well as in the domestic circle, and a diary has value in that it often explains the background, and pictures the forces at play beneath the surface. When we examine the political and mental upheavals of the day, we find that they are inevitable because they are basic in human nature, for the motives within man must be objectified before man can understand himself. The wise child makes his own toys, discovers his own absorptions, and practices the technique of his own expressions. Mankind as a unit is the maturing effort of the child. Children are like grown people, for the experience of others is never of any service to them.

Keeping a diary encourages one to be accurate in observing the play of events which are continually in action about us. It has been said of Plato, Socrates and Aristotle that they are "secretaries of nature." What we write down usually remains in our memory, and it is well to refresh the memory for she is indolent in her sluggish moods. Nature has a mysterious way of stirring our interest. Walt Whitman has said, "To me every hour of the light and dark is a miracle, every inch of cubic space is a miracle." And, Ludwig Tieck tells us, "Love has no winters, No, No. It is and remains the sunlight of spring."

Edward Dyer writes:

> My mind to me a kingdom is;
>   Such present joys therein I find,
> That it excels all other bliss
>   That earth affords or grows by kind;
> Though much I want which most would have,
> Yet still my mind forbids to crave.

It is well to look into the world, examine little forms of Life, and try to image with what spirit they meet their problems. If the little worms or bugs ever think, their only idea is food; if an angel looked down on us and read our thoughts, what would he see? The universe that lies beyond is thickly veiled from our eyes, but we may easily guess that there are degrees of knowledge concealed there which make our own very

little loftier than that of the wriggling worm. We do
not know what electricity is, but that does not prevent
us from harnessing and using it for service. So also are
forces beyond our mentality which can be utilized in
forming our experiences. We feel that impressions are
made on our minds, and somehow we can take hold on
the unknown, and in this mental flight we rise to heights
far beyond the range of our bodily sensations. Philosophy does not know what sensations really are, and
psychology can give no explanation of the nature of
experience, but that does not prevent us from feeling
sensations and knowing experience. Mystery is not a
word to frighten us; life would be lacking in zest if it
were missing. The beautiful, the romantic, and the
poetic, is the halo we weave around the commonplace
things which stimulate something in us. Arthur Edding-
ton says, "In the mystic sense of the creation around
us, in the expression of art, in a yearning towards God,
the soul grows upward and finds the fulfilment of something implanted in its nature." This is not illusion, it is
experience, and on the rocks of that experience we
build the house which gives the soul a home. We can
have no sensuous knowledge of things which transcend
the senses and are made of substances that are spiritual.
It is the spiritual within us which responds to the
spiritual that is in others, whether they be incarnate in
flesh or have ascended beyond the limitations of the
physical.

No great revolutionary truth ever came to a single
individual mind; it touches those first who are nearest
to it, for truth is a substance which cannot be confined to one receptacle or monopolized by one man.
There are degrees of truth: encyclopedic knowledge is
a common possession, it may be true or untrue; scientific knowledge can be verified by instruments, it re-

mains true until some new discovery excludes its possibility; spiritual truth reveals itself to the mind of
him who seeks to do justice and show mercy. Its veracity is known in the practice of it, and it becomes a
matter of experience. It is advisable to define what
truth we mean, and to bear in mind that it must be
judged within the sphere of its own connotations.
Truth is the eye of love, for without its lens love is
blind. We perceive truth according to our love, and
affection has three levels of operation. The scientific
affection discovers the laws and rules of the cosmic
universe and employs its facts for utilitarian ends;
the moral affections develop truth from personal experience, and from the lessons committed to us by the
masters who have passed on; the inward intuitions
perceive truth which is revealed to them from the
super-world. The first are factual truths; the second
are ethical truths, and the third are spiritual truths. No
fact or truth appeals to the reason, or becomes permanent with men, unless it is an answer to the affection for
knowing that it is so, and thus as a means for controlling behavior, or achieving some desired end. Our
human method is to explore causes from effects, first
analytically so that we may arrive at conclusions, and
then synthetically so that we can attain a desired
result. The mind ascends from natural facts verified
in the world to the moral truths verified by practice,
and then to the spiritual verities tested by experience.
This is the legendary ladder of Jacob; first the angels
of affection ascend, and having risen above the earth
and confirmed their observations, they descend with
the new light, and act according to their superior
knowledge.

If we wish to employ ourselves to advantage and to
secure satisfactions, it is necessary to have some su-

preme interest in Life, and not to merely feed in and
on the trivial husks which the daily grind attempts to
throw against the door of our mind. The principal
cause of futility is the lack of organization around
some central purpose. Clear thinking demands perse-
verance in blocking the fantasies of the mind from
crushing and stifling reflection in sustained thought.
A popular book is usually one which excoriates some
elect class of people, or caters to the depraved taste of
the mentally indolent, because they have more obses-
sions than ideas, and more persuasions than convictions. It is so easy to worship some self-elected hero
and then lose one's naturalness in imitating him. Conversation about little things may be pleasant for the
moment, but it is often a thought-hindering insincerity.
Genuine thought is the ability to distinguish between
ideas, for ideas present to the mind much more than
words. Our idea of a man is the composite of all that
we have heard or seen of him, and the idea has in it
all of the details. When thinking of men and compar-
ing them we form chains of ideas. It is these associated
ideas which construct judicious thought. The more complete our facts are, the more perfect is the idea. A
person clarifies his idea of the universe by studying
astronomy, physics and mathematics.

The person who begins to think seriously has started
on a road which will bring him many surprises and
not a few delights. He will appreciate what Lord
Balfour has said:

Our highest truths are but half-truths.
Think not to settle down forever in any truth.
Make use of it as a tent in which to pass a summer's night,
But build no house of it, or it will be your tomb.
When you find the old truth irksome and confining,
When you first have an inkling of its insufficiency,

And begin to descry a dim counter-truth looming up beyond,
Then weep not, but give thanks:
It is the Lord's voice, whispering,
"Take up thy bed and walk."

Memory holds the impression of the images received from the imagination. It is in the correctness and relation, the arrangement and employment, of these images that intelligent perception is developed. Philosophy is often inconclusive because when considering the nature of truth it becomes involved in terms, and each school rests content in contemplating its definitions. The ideas and truths are beclouded and lost in a technique which satisfies intellectual glory. What we call common sense is the ability to perceive civil and moral ideas, in which are the affairs and larger concerns of men and society. Undeveloped ideas are contaminated with errors, and are like moving shadows, which in our illusions distort themselves into all kinds of unreasonable forms. The credulous and visionary pursue these illusions as realities.

The potential structure of truth is in the individual affection. When the outer fact answers to the inner thought it is like a seed responding to the light and heat of the sun; it takes on form, and color, and fragrance. The world has no beauty beyond the beauty which its objects can awaken in us. The curious child who holds a shell to his ear must learn that it does not echo the roar of the sea; its music is the surging flow of the child's own blood stream. It is only when we penetrate the veil of the material that we see the miracle of Life at work with its tools. The smallest insect and flower grow in beauty and perfection the more deeply they are explored. The beauty is in the orderly arrangement of their several parts, because this order is imposed on them by untrammeled Life which seeks to perform a use through them. The ability to see the inner meaning increases according to the degree of our observation. The artist by practice acquires a keenness and precision of sight; the musician cultivates a sensitiveness of the ear to sound, and the surgeon manipulates his instruments with delicacy of touch in the performance of his duties. Dr. Helen Keller perhaps sees more beauty in nature, although her sight is lost, than many others who go blindly through the world with both eyes open.

Often the best training a student gets is that obtained outside the schoolroom, for native ability has a way of finding the things which satisfy its cravings. The fact that something within us is continually trying to assert itself is one of the phenomena of personal experience. The pity is that so many are deaf to the voices which cry from their souls and blind to the beauty which appeals on every side to their inner vision. It is what a person draws from his inner-self that is of prime importance in education, and the cultivated inner-self often causes us to realize that we are greater than we know or admit. The cosmic order of nature is one of the great marvels that fascinates the scientific mind, and this order challenges and condemns the disorder which is rampant in man and discordant in all of his social systems. Man has perfected no government, no laws of justice and equity, because he has not evolved order within himself.

This world, insofar as man is concerned, is a universe which inspires thoughts and feelings, and these are of vastly more importance than the objects that provoke them. Actually, we do not live in the world; it is but an outer shell, for each of us moves in the chambers of his own thought and love. The body with its five or six senses gives man contact with visible things, but the body seeks this contact because it is urged on by the soul, for the soul must develop and grow in order to achieve its greater destiny. Animals that feed on material things grow fat and move unconsciously to their own doom, for they become food for the body of man and thus perform a use in providing for his education. Many of our self-appointed advisers attempt to tell us that man has no future beyond this world, ignoring all the salient signs and forgetting all of the facts, for it is self-evident that man is building character and personality, and that these substantial creations are not limited by the material. Many of the finest characters this world has ever produced have signally failed in everything that the world regards as valuable. Our standards never fit them; our histories fail to record their names; they live in realms that overtop our world, and their creative powers are lost in arts which escape the eye and ear of the physical. Who can say that they do not count in the midst of that universe which is immeasurably above this in splendor, in possibilities, and perfection of its related forms? These souls are outside our categories, and above our standards. History as it was and is written is not a complete or true record of human achievement, for it pictures only the material side.

> Here's to the men who lose!
> What though their work be e'er so nobly planned,
> And watched with zealous care,
> No glorious halo crowns their efforts grand,
> Contempt is failure's share.

There are scientists who devote many years to verify one set of facts, and others who sacrifice health and comfort for the benefit of mankind. To know the secrets of nature, one must first learn the laws of her behavior before he can utilize the force he has discovered. Desire stimulates zeal for facts, and the facts lead to uses. The individual who wishes to act honestly and justly first learns the difference between right and wrong, and governs himself accordingly. The person who aspires to the knowledge of the spiritual must learn the truths which govern and control the spirit. All of this takes time, and some existences are too brief for both learning and practice.

Civil laws need no enactment for those who control conduct that harmonizes with the ideals of Jesus. The penalties inflicted by law are aimed at the unsocial and to beget in them a sense of fear. Legal tribunals are not necessarily courts of justice, for they decide human-made laws and the decisions are colored by prejudice and political necessity. The State regards marriage as a contract which legalizes the breeding of children, and protects their rights, ignoring the truth that marriage blends the inherent qualities of a man and a woman into a unit of relationship that has eternal possibilities. There is a marriage of male and female qualities in every created thing, and from this union develops a new form of superior usefulness. There is a marriage of truth and love in the human mind. Marriage therefore begets new types.

Marriage begets a new type of love which would be undiscovered if the world contained men and women who did not seek a mutual companionship. Marriage produces a new power, beauty and effectiveness. It encourages tolerance, humility, and the sense of service for others. It begins on the low level of sex attraction, but it rises to the consecration and spiritualization of high ideals. It makes the partners better citizens, gives them a conscientious understanding of human relations, and helps them in undertaking work for the good of others. In this relationship the propagation of children belongs to this world, but the propagation of new ideas, of new understandings, and new purposes, belongs to the next world. The main driving force of the world is love, and women can express this power much better than men; love needs intelligence and masculine strength as a control, and marriage is the meeting ground of this union. Love without wisdom is passion or folly; intellectuality without love is harsh, cold and forbidding. Life has made all things complementary, and until they are wisely conjoined they cannot create new channels or find the new outlets. The enduring quality in man is love and intelligence, and the closer they are conjoined the more fit they are to survive the change between death and life. Tennyson has said:

> For woman is not undeveloped man,
> But diverse; could we make her as a man,
> Sweet Love were slain: his dearest bond is this
> Not like to like, but like in difference:
> Yet in long years liker they must grow.

It is said that reason can see the folly of unverified reason, but reason, to be true to itself, must not attempt to limit the evidence to material facts, because reason itself is not material. She has no qualities that can be measured by physical analysis, no structure that conforms to mathematical rules. The only visible knowledge we have of reason is seen in the effects and results which she produces. Reason cannot be judged by the evidence of the senses, for she nowhere makes contact with the sensuous.

The remarkable feature of the trained mind is that it can examine the workings of its own organism. It does this by means of an internal light which shines down on the functioning planes of its own organism, and because the spirit of man, in the preservation of its own entity, is superior to the mind through which it seeks expression. Even though the mind were paralyzed, the spirit preserves its contacts with the material and the spiritual worlds. The mind is not always a true index of the spirit; even philosophers have souls. When it is said that we are placed in a mysterious universe, let it be added that we have intuitions which can fathom the secret of the mysterious. George Herbert suggests that we need to know ourselves and this understanding can be acquired in solitude and contemplation:

By all means use sometimes to be alone,
Salute thyself; see what thy soul doth wear;
Dare to look in thy chest; for 'tis thine own,
And tumble up and down what thou findest there.

Of what use are the impressions we gather, the encyclopedic facts and rambling informations, unless they are coördinated into tools of personal expression? In this method they become part of ourselves, for they are thus embodied in act and practice. Our inner reason assembles the incoherent bits of knowledge and shapes them in clusters and groups. Particles of sand can be melted by heat to form glass, and a silver backing produces the mirror; just so do these particles of knowledge combine and fuse to mirror our affections and souls. Knowledge needs testing in the crucible of good use, and when so refined it makes man wise. Pythagoras and Plato had the idea of a force immaterial, but inseparable from matter, which gave to matter its form and movement. The philosopher who argues that mind is not a thing in itself, separate and distinct from the material thing it contemplates, always reasons himself and his world out of existence as a logical conclusion. Because there is mystery and a universe, there is also a mind which can observe and solve the mystery, for every active force leaves tracks capable of detection. The scientific mind has been actively solving mysteries for two hundred years, and its methods are becoming more perfect in the practice. There are many miracles performed by the mind of man to-day; the miracles of scripture show how spiritual power solves the secrets of nature for its own revealing; science performs miracles for the benefit of human progress.

The German chemist, Stahl, in 1700, advanced the theory that the soul (anima) is the principle of Life, and that it not only forms the fetus in the womb, but also determines all of its activities. He contended that the soul is the source of all normal and abnormal phenomena, and that disease is due to some physical obstruction in the free action of the soul. The error of much modern philosophy consists in maintaining that the mind is swayed by physical forces and controlled by them. But, we cannot forget that the mind is not physical, it is not electrical, it is spiritual and moves in the sphere of the spirit. The mind feels love, it employs truth to control its affections and shape its thought, but neither love nor truth is material. There have always been two schools of thought; one claims that the physical is sovereign in man and that his mental experiences and states can be chemically and biologically defined; the other insists that there is a spirit quality which produces the phenomena of Life, and that the physical is *per se* lifeless, its activity is the invisible spirit working through it. These two ideas recur at periods, and change their garments and arguments to suit the new conditions. The one school contends that thought is in the mind, the other believes

that thought is in the brain; the latter have no faith in
life after death, the former say that man, as he is in
his mind, can never perish. The belief that the universe
is mechanical and without intelligent purpose is opposed by those who pursue their studies in the conviction that there is a master mind in control of all things.
Does the body heal itself, or is there some invisible
force which heals? Is the motion of the atom self-
generated, or is there a pure and invisible motion to
which it responds? No human eye has ever seen an
atom, we must accept its probability on faith; no one
has ever seen a thought, and its existence is a matter
of faith. Science, like religion, is largely built on faith,
because no work would be possible to man if he had
no faith in the reality of the unseen.

A serious thinker does not conceive the universe in
terms of personality because the center of his own
interests is his personality; he concludes that Life
must be Person because Life employs intelligence to
objectify its love. It is exactly the same principle of
action which makes a human being a man; deprive him
of this power and faculty, grant him a perfect physical
body, and yet he remains the animal. The fact that
much of our thinking is distorted and misdirected does
not prove in itself that the mind cannot some day
evolve a perfection which will revolutionize social systems and revitalize the world thought. Man is in the
making, poor stuff now, but there are endless possibilities. Our time is engaged in continually thinking of
ourselves, personal comfort and convenience, rather
than in doing our best for others and living our noblest.
We often refrain from thinking in lofty terms, and
attempt to hide beneath an invented ægis. Francis
Bacon thrusts his scalpel at the root of the trouble
when he says, "Does any man doubt, that if there were

taken out of men's minds vain opinions, false valuations, imaginations as one would, and the like, but it would leave the minds of a number of men poor, shrunken things full of melancholy and indisposition, and unpleasing to themselves."

Angela Morgan has visioned the force at work beneath our inner selves, in these words:

> When nature wants to mold a man
> To play the noblest part;
> When she yearns with all her heart
> To create so great and bold a man
> That all the world shall praise—
> Watch her method, watch her ways.
>
> How she bends, but never breaks,
> When his good she undertakes;
> How she uses whom she chooses,
> And with every purpose fuses him.
> By every art induces him
> To try his splendor out—
> Nature knows what she's about.

In the mental and emotional stream float many impressions and ideas, both good and bad, in seething confusion. Our minds are like shallow pools into which part of this confused water flows, and what remains may be clear fluid and sediment. Laurence Binyon says:

> Futurity flows toward me, all things flow
> Full-streaming, and ere a pulse beat they are bound
> In fixity that no repenting power can free;
> They are with Egypt and with Nineveh,
> Cold as a grave in the ground:
> And still, undated, all things flow toward me.

The germ-plasm within all creative work is the idea; gradually this idea expands, annexing its selected companions, until it becomes a mastering purpose that cannot be resisted. Louis Barye, the sculptor, plays with cats and watches their quick actions and changing moods, and out of these seemingly idle meditations come those treasured bronzes of lions and tigers that grace the marble halls of great museums. How can we develop this inner-self which has receptivities and possibilities that are mysteries even to ourselves? We can select the material which it feeds on by finding delight in the things which have meaning for us. A strain of music, or the fragrance of a flower, can revive states in our minds which reproduce all of their details. In periods of inspiration vast regions of our soul are revealed to us which have nothing in common with the barrenness of daily existence; our intellectual vision is keen and sensitive to the overtones and undertones of vibrating Life. As the words fly back and forth in conversation we read the speaker's motives like an open book. It is then that to him who in the love of nature seeks communion with her inner soul, she speaks a various language. We treasure our best thoughts on bits of paper, and, in the course of time, out of their ashes rises the phenix which scales the higher altitudes of thought.

All of us are creatures of emotion, rather than of intelligence, and in our human relations the feelings are involved. In passive and pensive moments we carry back to the altar of our affections all of our thoughts and acts to have them tested at her shrine.

We cannot live worthily without ideals. Our minds are sacred places, and the crude shoes of common soil must be removed if we expect to content ourselves within the glow of their fires. Ideals release us from the tyrannical consciousness of the crowd; they aid us in perceiving ourselves as we really are, our relation to other individuals, our perpetual forward movement, and our fidelity to the inner guide. We know a thing only by uniting ourselves to it, by assimilating it, by an inner penetration of it and ourselves. It gives itself to us, in the measure that we give ourselves to it. The mystic, Sufi, says, "Pilgrimage to the place of the wise is to escape the flame of separation." What shall we consciously seize upon, with what unite?

As the sculptor devotes himself to wood and stone
   I would devote myself to the living soul.
But I am solemnized by the thought that the sculptor cannot carve
   Either on wood or on stone, or on the living soul,
   Anything better than himself.
All the lines of my carving
   Will but reveal my own portrait.
Gazing at my hand, at my chisel, I shudder.
How long will it take for this human sculpture,
Which cannot be carved by me better, finer than my own soul,
   To escape? To escape from my pitiable and limited domain,
And to advance to the position of a carving of God?
Happily, there is a guide for me.
   It is he who has broken open the door of the sanctuary
And made a molten cast of God's portrait in his own flesh.

We know from personal experience that man is here in the world—a material world, consciously, and that there is something within him capable of reviewing all of his thoughts, words, deeds, and contacts with others of his kind. This human mind is the conscious side of his spirit; the spirit has contact with the invisible world, but of that contact man is unconscious while he is bound to the earth. He is conscious of the physical world because his body is a medium of sensation, and a mechanism by means of which he expresses his spirit in physical ways. It is to him what the piano is to Beethoven and what the laboratory is to Edison; the piano is not Beethoven and the laboratory is not Edison. The Benedictus of the Mass in D is an expression of Beethoven's spirit, and the electric lamp and phonograph are expressions of Edison's spirit, and these manifestations live after them.

The mind assents to nothing which is useless to spirit; it is our body and our needs that compel us to assume our world. There is a realm of essence, and the spirit has an intuition of those essences, immediate, changeless and absolute, and no skepticism can destroy them, because they are substantial. The spirit-mind turns from its animal sources and mechanical conditions to a contemplation of its own needs, and the spirit uses the thoughts and images which answer its desires. Science and religion are systems of symbols in the scheme of notations of the conditions of existence, and in them the spirit renders its values and aspirations. By this method the spirit-mind achieves a twofold harmony, the inner harmony of its intuitions, and the outer harmony between the body and its environment. Science is a disciplined symbolism in which the spirit, through the mind, learns to understand the conditions of its physical basis.

In experience, art and religion, values flower legitimately from the desires of the body, and their functional origin does not destroy them. The natural basis of values was created by man for himself because it has a relation to the activities of unconscious spirit. All of these world values are derived from man's needs as a psychological and social being. Art, religion and science are human attempts to relate his inner pattern to nature, for there is an intelligence somewhere capable of seeing all and knowing all. Because of the nature of his mind, conscious and unconscious, man has difficulty in comprehending reality as it is, and therefore assumes the existence of a spiritual measuring rod. Literature becomes interesting when it is adventurous, and unfolds new areas of experience, and the best books and best poems are yet to be written.

If we admit that there is a positive distinction between what man is in himself, mentally and spiritually, and what man appears to be in his physical appearance and acts, we may dismiss the materialistic speculations concerning the concordant action of cells as generators of thought. We can also avoid the entangling theories regarding his origin. He is here no matter how he arrived, and we are confronted by a condition and not a theory. We know that man has intuitions and perceptions that cannot be explained by the action of unintelligent cells and atoms. We can deny this, or affirm it, but in either case the decision is made not in man's bodily functions, but within his inner self, for that is the court of origins and final appeal. Mind is superior to matter, and the brain is not the mind.

> The senses folding thick and dark
>   About the stifled soul within,
> We guess diviner things beyond,
>   And yearn to them with yearning fond;
> We strike out blindly to a mark
>   Believed in, but not seen.

The roots of all great thinking and noble acting lie deep in the mind itself, and not in the dry shuffling of mere reasoning. All creative work is inspired by high ideals trained to function through experience. Intuitive perception, which is spiritual wisdom, is a type of achievement that belongs to the highest range of mental activity. The great scientific and religious discoveries are due to the inventive genius of the creative thinkers, and not to the plodding processes of the unenlightened mind. Creative work is not blind imitation or mechanical repetition, it is synthetic insight which advances by leaps. A new truth, startling in its strangeness, comes into being suddenly, born of the intense and concentrated interest in the problem; with the controlling new idea comes a wealth of coördinated detail which immediately assumes a proper order and forms a perfect whole. These flashes of wondrous insight are less the product of reasoning than of revelation. Mr. Needham, in *The Sceptical Biologist*, says, "The fact that the scientific investigator works 50 percent of his time by non-rational means is quite insufficiently recognized . . . and often the most successful investigators are quite unable to give an account of their reasons for doing a specific experiment, or for placing side by side two apparently unrelated facts. Again, one of the most salient traits in the character of the successful scientific worker is the capacity for knowing that a point is proved when it would not appear to be proved to an outside intelligence functioning in a purely rational manner; thus the investigator feels that some proposition is true, and proceeds without waiting or wasting time for formal proof. The scientific worker operates to a high degree unconsciously, as it were, like the builders of coral reefs."

The ability to discover the meaning of unrelated facts is the spirit-mind's intuitive grasp of the dynamic principle which enables the investigator to organize the facts successfully. Bergson has dealt with this problem: it is generally supposed that scientific discovery is reached by conceptual synthesis, but the insight does not arise if we are not familiar with the facts of the case, and the successful practice of intuition requires previous study and assimilation of the facts and laws, and we may take it that great intuitions arise out of

an understanding of the problem and its adjustment to
the inner desire to bring it into effect. Inventions are
therefore by intuition, and later proved by logic. The
intuition cannot be gained by mere intellectual effort,
though it is equally true that it cannot succeed without
it. The essence of things cannot resist the concentrated
attack of the whole mind, and intuitive ideas are given
birth in those deep silences which interrupt our busy
moments. In them the mind is under the control of the
spirit, and the deeper consciousness grows and becomes
intensely aware of the nature of the object. On the
relaxation of intellect, the truth shapes itself from
within and leaps forth as a spark from the fire. When
the flash occurs we feel it to be true, and find that it
lights up the puzzles and paradoxes and places them
in luminous atmosphere.

"The spirit bloweth where it listeth, and thou canst
not tell whence it cometh and whither it goeth." It is
therefore that inspiration does not deprive us of reason and then takes possession, for inspiration is not a
substitute for thought, it is a challenge to our intelligence. So long as we are lost in the detail of sense and
intellect our soul is unresponsive, but when we are—

> laid asleep
> In body and become a living soul
> While with an eye made quiet by the power
> Of harmony, and the deep power of joy
> We see into the life of things.

Poetry is a form of expression, a realization of the
meaning of common life by living it more intensely, a
flinging of oneself on it, moving into its rhythm and
seeing into it. True poetry, which is rich with suffering
and experience, has the fullness and mystery, the depth
and authority of life itself. Carlyle says, "Poetic creation, what is this too, but seeing the thing sufficiently?

The word that will describe the thing follows of itself from such clear, intense sight of the thing." The creative spirit and its activity are interior to the conscious mind, but the latter feels itself to be inspired and raised above its normal power by the breath of the spirit.

The poet believes that his work is due not to his intellectual skill or imaginative boldness, but to what he calls his inspiration, since it comes to him and fades out regardless of his inclination. The power is more unconscious than conscious: "They remember moments when a new light or reviving force appeared to stream upon them coming whence it would, from the presence or the thoughts of the living or the departed, from intercourse with nature, from the heights of personal joy or the obscure deeps of pain." Dante says, "I am one who, when love inspires, take note and as he dictates within me I express myself." This experience is not confined to poets, for many persons in various situations have knowledge of moments when the spirit and the mind are fused in procreative heat. Alfred North Whitehead, professor of philosophy at Harvard, says, "There are two routes of creative passage from the physical occasion; one is toward another physical occasion, and the other is towards a derivative reflective occasion. The physical route links together physical occasions as successive temporal incidents in the life of the body. The other route links this bodily life with a correlative mental life. A mental occasion is an ultimate fact in the spiritual world, just as a physical occasion of blind perceptivity is an ultimate fact in the physical world. There is an essential reference from one world to the other."

> Mind sees by spirit: Body moves by mind:
> Divorced from spirit, both way-wildered fall—
> Leader and led, the blindfold and the blind.

CHAPTER IV

THE MIND AS AN ORGANISM

FOR those who are interested in the mysterious processes of life a knowledge of the human mind and its operations is an appealing subject. Solomon, who prayed not for long life, nor for riches, nor for the bodies of his enemies, but for understanding to discern judgment, said, "Wisdom hath builded her house, she hath hewn out her seven pillars; she hath killed her beasts; she hath mingled her wine; she hath also furnished her table. She hath sent forth her maidens: she crieth upon the highest places of the city, Whoso is simple, let him turn in hither: as for him that wanteth understanding, she saith to him, Come, eat of my bread, and drink of the wine which I have mingled. Forsake the foolish and live; and go in the way of understanding."

William Wordsworth, who knew that wisdom comes from world contacts, said,

> He is happiest who hath power,
> To gather wisdom from every flower,
> And wake his heart in every hour,
> To pleasant gratitude.

The mind gathers its delights from many sources, it builds its house of many materials, and it governs its realm in sobriety and order.

> So work the honey bees;
> Creatures that, by a rule of nature, teach
> The act of order to a peopled kingdom.
> They have a queen, and officers of sorts;

Where some, like magistrates, correct at home;
Others, like merchants, venture trade abroad;
Others, like soldiers, armed in their stings,
Make boot upon the summer's velvet buds;
Which pillage they, with merry march, bring home
To the tent-royal of their empress,
Who, busied in her majesty, surveys
The singing masons building roofs of gold;
The civil citizens kneading up the honey;
The poor mechanic porters crowding in
Their heavy burdens at her narrow gate;
The sad-eyed justice, with his surly hum,
Delivering o'er to executors pale
The lazy, yawning drone.

Any study is vital and productive of satisfaction which throws new light on human activities, the impulses and motives which move human beings to do ordinary acts and extraordinary deeds. If we could gain a knowledge of the hidden ideas and beliefs, their effect on behavior, and the determining influence on human relations and social systems, we could construct a definite picture of tessellated mosaics as a basis for a more complete study. A scientific analysis would show that the course of human action is determined at the source of mental and emotional energy. We must discover the potential possibilities and limits of the human material before general rules can be formulated for the guidance of human conduct in the field of legislation and government, for social affairs concern human beings only. Man has a body and mind, which are intro-active, and granted that the body is continually re-creating itself, then we must admit that a similar and more refined evolution is progressing in mental characteristics.

Man, as the most perfect of living organisms, has the power of sensation and the faculty of learning, and in so far as his innate potentialities and external reality permit, both worlds are his to experience. It depends upon the approach to life whether we succeed in attaining our complete expression; for the ordinary man uses his experience for practical and utilitarian ends, while others command their experience as an end in itself. Some have the power to penetrate the surface of experience and transform it into something above the ordinary. Thoughts, actions and endeavors are open to various interpretations. The difference is in the man and his approach, for he can produce a perfect record of experience in creative art and beauty. To be more alive, more susceptible to both worlds, enhances world values, develops superior capacities, and encounters greater responsibilities.

Dr. Frank Crane said that mad men win, for "a man can never attain his highest ideal unless he goes slightly insane." He gives an example of the German physicist, Julius Robert von Mayer, who propounded the doctrine of the conservation of energy. He labored under the delusion of grandeur, and in his provincial town of Heilbronn was considered as insane, and everyone attempted to exercise a spiritual guardianship over him. The world's greatest dramas picture the struggle of the soul to free itself from hindering limitations in an effort to find satisfactory expression. Shakespeare, Molière, Ibsen, Swinburne, and others knew the power of personality, and others, like Strindberg, the Swedish dramatist, were themselves on the fringe of insanity. Queen Christina of Sweden abdicated the throne so that she might give expression to her artistic nature unfettered by the forced and formal duties of state. There is something in the soul of a great person that craves its fulfilled ideals.

Psychologists have made the mistake in the past of

using the introspective method exclusively, of analyzing and describing conscious states by this one method. They sought for a line of conduct which would produce the maximum of pleasure and the minimum of pain; whereas men are moved by a variety of impulses and motives. Mankind as a unit is seldom reasonable; in fact, behavior is very inconsistent, and it is advisable to know why the unreasonable persists. Science advances to its knowledge by observation and examination of the phenomena of nature and of living things. In the study of psychic phenomena a doctrine of human motives must be formulated, a science of the human mind in all of its aspects and modes of functioning; to do this it is essential to observe the behavior of men under all known conditions of association, of health, and of disease. It is well to remember that human beings are more important, more everlasting, than machines. There is an insistent demand for new aspects and perspectives. There are fundamental elements, innate tendencies of thought and action, which constitute the native basis of mind. The adult mind is molded by the influence of the social environment, and in turn it reacts to and reforms that environment to its own thought. The native tendencies which coöperate in determining the course of life become organized gradually in complex systems, but they remain unchanged in their essential attributes. Social psychology must explain how, granting the native capacities and propensities of the human mind, all the complex life of society is shaped by them, and how the reaction affects the development and comportment of the individual.

Highly organized society and government call for a high standard of morals, conduct and character. Doctor Rashdell has said, "the raw material, so to speak, of virtue and of vice is the same, *viz.*, desires which in themselves, abstracted from the higher self, are neither moral nor immoral, but simply non-moral." The moralization of the individual is essential, for purely egoistic tendencies are often stronger, especially in youth, than are the altruistic tendencies. Men are much more easily led by their inclinations than they are by their aspirations.

When we come to a study of the human mind and its relation to that part of the body known as the brain we encounter difficulties, for very little actual work has been done in this department of science. It is true that science must limit its researches to facts, and that microscopic and chemical laboratory tests cannot be made of psychic substances which do not so submit themselves. Science at first postulated the atom because it was difficult to explain the universe by any other known means. It is equally true that we must regard the psychic mind as a distinct organism because there are mental phenomena which cannot be otherwise explained.

The Greek philosopher, Democritus, living about the year 300 B.C., propounded the theory of a universe by atoms in motion. The atomic theory therefore dates back some 2,000 years. Both Epicurus and Lucretius further developed the theory, but it remained in the field of speculation until modern science took it up seriously. And in like manner, the early Greek philosophers had a theory of mind, and it has continued as a subject of speculation to the present day. The subject has often been mystified and clouded in philosophical terms. There is something about it which has an appeal, and modern technical psychologists have done much to make the matter popular, especially in showing how it could be used in salesmanship and business. John Dewey, evidently with this phase in mind, has said in some of his University lectures, "Even now, popular psychology is a mass of cant, of slush, and of superstition worthy of the most flourishing days of the medicine man."

We expect too much when it is imagined that the general public can be interested in the discoveries of pure science, or be familiar with the particulars of great achievements. They have never understood the true principles within the Darwinian theory. Evolution became popular when it offered an avenue of escape. The mass of men instinctively feels that human nature has never succeeded, that political governments have failed in meeting their requirements, that scholars have never understood all of the truth, and that there is a certain element of futility in life. Men have always sought to escape their responsibilities, and anything which offered an excuse or alibi was welcomed. The evolution theory, as conceived by the mass of men, permitted a shifting of this burden to hereditary traits and to the ancestral ape. The Mendelian theory became popular at a later date because it confirmed the common idea.

It is needless to say that neither the Darwinian nor Mendelian doctrines, when properly understood, encouraged this view. What really counts is that the general public put its own construction and interpretation upon the matter. The public obtains its information from daily papers which publish tabloid forms of news, containing none of the details and omitting the argument, but written in sensational style. The genuine scientist is a humble worker, with an open and receptive mind, not seeking publicity either for himself or for his discoveries. The general public does not understand these theories; they are given fanciful catch-words, which some persons use as a pretense to cover superficial thinking.

That there is in the background of the human mind a vague idea that men have always failed in their political governments is indicated by well-established symptoms. There is a constant effort on the part of men, both ignorant and intelligent, to devise some utopian form of government. There are many small communities in the world where social panaceas are being tried out by their devotees. Within the larger governments there is a continual shifting of political parties and rulers. The bibliography on this one phase of sociology is very extensive. All of these known facts bear on their face the evidence of a universal unrest and discontent. Herbert Spencer could compare the best of social governments to nothing more perfect than the organization found in the structure of the lower forms of animal life. And it is known that these have a short duration of life, which is equally true of political systems.

We have sufficient scientific material on which to pattern a greatly improved type of government, but society does not begin in types of government, but in the minds of human beings. If thoughts are vague and inconclusive, and desires uncontrolled, no social fabric can endure. Many untenable conclusions prevail because the persons have not examined all of the available data. It is known that men will contend most vehemently for ideas and theories which they least understand, but which have the approved stamp of some highly esteemed authority. The pure scientist is not dogmatic; he holds an open mind for he knows that the theories held to-day may be overthrown in a few years. There are a number of opinions on the exact nature of mind, but there is no difference of opinion as to its importance in shaping human conduct. There are some who contend that the mind is mechanical and chemical, and that mind and brain are synonymous terms. There were learned men in former times who believed that the soul resided in the heart, and that the secret animal fluid flowed through the middle channel of the nerves. Fanciful beliefs persist with persons who will not concede the consequences of a complete analysis of known facts. In the beginning of any scientific study there are many conflicting opinions, inevitable where any guesswork enters.

Many volumes have been written on the subject of the mind and on the art of thinking, which deal largely with fragmentary mental phenomena, but do not examine the structure and functional organization of mind. Some authors speak of making the mind, as though the mind were a creation of man. It may be safely concluded that the mind is not made, for the mind is the man himself, as will be shown in this and the next chapter. The mind is potentially human. It may be developed and trained, but it cannot be constructed of chemical matter. The mind is spirit, and without it no one can develop personality or claim to be human. The human body can be developed and trained, for the single biological cell is the germ of its life. In the same manner the mind can be developed and trained from the simple structure of its spiritual and individual germ or norm.

Modern scientific knowledge had its beginning in the quest for truth amidst the confusions thrust upon the world by the speculations of the middle ages. Psychic science must begin in the same way, cutting through all of the mysticism which fake mediums and spiritists of the Conan Doyle type have elaborated for commercial ends. The word *psychic* has valuable connotations, and we must discard the word "metaphysics" which has nothing to do with mentality, but is rather a dialectic philosophical speculation. In his poem *Ulalume*, Edgar Allen Poe says:

> Here once, through an alley Titanic
>> Of cypress, I roamed with my Soul—
>> Of cypress, with Psyche, my Soul.
> These were the days when my heart was volcanic
>> As the scoriac rivers that roll.
> Thus I pacified Psyche and kissed her,
>> And tempted her out of her gloom,
>> And conquered her scruples and gloom.

Fabricius and Harvey were not content to accept the theories of the blood which prevailed in their day, 1600–1630, and they worked diligently to discover the secrets of the cardiac system. Faraday, in the same way, began by examining the phenomena and nature of electricity and animal magnetism. In examining the structure and nature of mind we are on new ground, and only the truth within the old theories can be utilized. The spirit of objective and detached inquiry will in itself remove the antiquated prejudices and traditional religious ideas, which have become fixed in human thought and are therefore difficult to eradicate. The best and purest in religion will be helpful, for religion stands in relation to our quest very much in the same attitude that astrology holds to scientific astronomy; where philosophy stood in its relation to science, and where the herb doctor stood as to modern medical thought.

Every important study has confused beginnings, it has its swaddling clothes which must be outgrown. Speaking of the cell organization of the human body, a recent writer has said, "We are forced to assume the existence of some sort of controlling and coördinating principle outside the units themselves and superior to them. If these units constitute the physico-chemical basis of life, then this controlling principle, since it is an essential feature of life, must of necessity be something which is not physico-chemical in nature." Mental life must be traced to origins which are superior and prior to the mechanism of the bodily cells.

Modern psychology can be said to have begun seriously in the year of 1880 A.D., when it was freed from philosophy and religion. The beginners dealt mostly with parts of the mental activity, like the early physiologists who contented themselves with partial studies. For instance, the pituitary gland, which is so dominant in bodily growth, was neglected until recently, although its importance was acknowledged some 150 years ago by writers on Physiology. To avoid these mistakes, the general construction of the mind, and its operations as a whole should have consideration. We can gain some conception of the structure of the mind from our knowledge of the structure of the physical body, with which it is in accord. The mind has its functioning parts, just as the human body has its distinct yet coordinating systems. Memory, which by its impressions is close to the material, is a well-defined mental system, and its functions can be explained. Above the memory and superior to it is the faculty of reason, where judgments and opinions are formed. Within and prior to the reason is a finer system which may for convenience be called the illuminated intellect. These three systems depend one upon the other, and the coördination between them is active in ways similar to the functions of the systems of the physical body.

Let us examine some of the proofs which testify to the fact that the mind is an organism distinct from that of the physico-chemical human body. One of these proofs is education. No degree of education will improve the working of the cells of the human body. They are in no manner affected by education, nor do they function differently in the body of an intellectual man than they do in the ignorant and illiterate. Education, therefore, is solely confined to the operations of the human mind. Another proof is in the testimony of experience, for no amount of experience will change the chemical content or operation of physical cells. Living cells in an infant or child are just as perfect in their work as in the man of vast experience. Experience is registered in the mind, and by it the mind can become developed and cultured.

It will be said that no one disputes the existence of mind, and this may be true, but it is contended by some that the mind is part of the physical organism, and until this is disproved little headway can be made. For the mind is as distinct from the physical as is the material universe from the domain of thought and love. Both the external world and the internal mind are distinct from the human body, but they have a fixed and permanent relation to it. It is for this reason that the relationship must be established by defining the organic structure of mind and to show that it is not cellular or physical.

Just as conditions in the external world have power to influence the chemical reaction of physical cells, so also do conditions of mind have power to change and influence them. Grief, anger and fear are psychic operations, and it is well known that they have an immediate effect on the nerve and muscular systems. Conditions in the blood can be altered by states of mind. A charitable disposition toward others, confidence and enjoyment in personal duties, stimulate and purify the blood. Psychiatrists recognize the connection between mind and body, and their therapeutic practice is based on the knowledge that diseases are created by mental states. The often used term, "psychosis," has connotations which define an abnormal state of mind. Psychoneurosis means that the mind and nerves are equally involved. It is known from personal experience that thought has a direct effect on the action of the heart and lungs. Fear causes the muscles to contract around the blood ducts and is shown in the pallid skin, while anger flushes and rushes the blood and excites the respiration. Consciousness, both of fear and of anger, belongs to the operation of the mind, and a sense of wrong doing, or of false statement, will so vibrate the heart action that the agitation can be mechanically measured. It is also true that persons under mental stress can be psychically assisted by the action of another person's mind. In human associations this form of assistance is far more frequent than we imagine. A mentally distressed child will come to its mother to be soothed and freed of its anxieties. It is not the physical cells of the mother which effect these alleviations, but the organized mind of that person. The evidences of psychic telepathy are too well verified to be ignored.

It is astonishing that so little consideration has been given to the phase of study which defines the mind as an independent organism. When we accept the doctrine of the psyche as mind, we must postulate a psychic realm or world in which mind operates. In view of all of the consequences involved, there is a scientific reluctance to face this problem, for science is limited in its efforts to the realm of matter. If we are to take up the problem of sociology in a scientific way we are compelled to examine and analyze the realm of mind. If religion desires to call the psychic realm the spiritual world, there need be no quarrel over terms. The name or label is immaterial; what we must recognize is the fact of such a realm as the only one possible for mental phenomena. The editors of the *Encyclopædia Britannica* probably regarded the subject as disputed, for there is no mention of either the spiritual or the mental world or realm. When the editors came to the subject of supernaturalism they confined the text to the matter of charlatanry, something which is decidedly irrelevant. These facts are mentioned to show that the subject of a mental or psychic realm, as a thing distinct and definite, has not yet entered seriously into the common literature. Our light has so far been pellucid rather than lucid, and we require a new technology of the mental functions.

What primarily differentiates people is the active factor which is dynamic in the individual. There may be several urges which are latent and potential, but it is the individual active factor which generates reactions in both mind and body. William James, the Harvard psychologist, recognized in his lectures and propounded in his books the unconscious as a vital power house stimulating and directing human action. Every one can know from experience that there is an insistent urge of the individual ego to express itself, and this it does wisely or unwisely, and in the effort the known and hidden processes of the mind play their part. We regard inspiration as a mental process of unknown origin, and it will be shown later that a light from the interior mind is thrown upon those things which a man knows, believes, and loves, and from this light on knowledge he is inspired.

Psychology speaks of fixations, complexes, reflexes, and involuntary compulsions, and these are psychic barriers due to retarded and defective mind development. These hindrances have their parallel in the human organism where organs or parts of the body are incapable of carrying their load, due to undernourishment. Much of the ignorance prevailing in society is regarded either as criminal or is excused, when the truth would show that it is a case of arrested or constricted development of the mental functions. During the period of childhood knowledge never comes from inside the mind, but arises in external object phenomena. The mental growth may be arrested at any time, due to family, to position or environment. Parents, in indirect ways, may easily lead a child to believe that he is not bright, and he will govern himself accordingly.

The important decisions in life frequently spring from obscure impulses of passion, ignorantly staged or controlled. Only with the educated person can we expect decisions arrived at from ample consideration and specified plan. All of this shows how necessary is the training of the mind. Another factor which influences life is the love of self, or ego-worship. It will be shown that affection and desire are powerful functions of the mind, and that they crystallize the substance of thought into definable forms. Love of ego is a form-fixing element, and the removal of these fixations is painful and frequently very slow. The cure is in converting the ego fixation to a love of the community, from a self-centered position to the larger external organization.

When we examine the sex love we find that the mind, wholly detached from concurring sense perceptions, can excite the hormones of the sex glands and conspire to the individual's physical ruin. The mind often influences the sex organs in dreams and during sleep. It is habitual to regard all of the deeper feelings as desires which must be satisfied, and it is only the trained mind that can distinguish between them and subject them to control. It is the untrained mind which commits the grosser moral follies; although an abnormal intellect can do greater damage to the body. Some writers on psycho-physics often exaggerate the influence of sex instincts on the mental states. Perhaps this is due to their patients, who are victims of sex repressions which have become chronic. The sex instinct is both natural and normal to man. No doubt, less than 1 per cent of the population is actually abnormally afflicted. It must be remembered that the sex organs are most insistent with those between the ages of fifteen and fifty years of age, and this excludes automatically a large percentage of the population. Persons who are oversexed usually exhaust their sex energies in early life, and the passions cool or are controlled. It must also be conceded that all of the passion is not harmful, for children are born, either legitimately or illegitimately, and the child is not responsible for the causes which brought it into the world. The illegitimate child does not suffer hereditarily from the sexual misdeeds of its parents. Sex thoughts are under continual excitement, in which the stage, literature, private conversation, openly or by innuendo, are involved. If these excitants were removed, it is questionable whether society would be much disturbed by this one passion.

True psycho-pathology does not set the mind opposite to the body, but as something inter-related with it. Much of the studies of former times has been too onesided. The physico-chemical reactions and functions are directly related to the mind. Claude Bernard thinks that the day will come when physiologist, psychologist, philosopher, and poet will speak the same language and then understand each other. It may come when we understand the full play of life, when the archaic and hereditary are separated from the organic, and when the narcistic self is understood in its relation to the social order. We humans are in this world for a purpose, and to idly drift is criminal, for we can from experience and education direct our course wisely.

A large proportion of our archaic lore is devoted to dreams, the German traumerei. The dream was considered as a medium between the organic mind and the organic body; therefore it was regarded as an infallible prophet. Much of modern psychosis is devoted to dream interpretation, in which the dream and impression states of childhood are sought out, but the symbols are arbitrarily classified according to the skill of the interpreter. This is not strictly scientific, and leaves much to the imagination of the operator. The dream is also regarded as an indication of warfare between intuition and repression. The defect in many civil and moral laws is in the repression of insistent cravings instead of directing them into moral and social channels. These repressions are said to expose themselves in dreams, and back of the dream is a craving which speaks the symbol language, and unconsciously suggests solutions by which the chain of bondage may be broken. In the study of dreams the telepathic and prophetic type of communication also receives attention. All of this study of dreams goes to prove that the active, functioning mind continues or overlaps the activities of the bodily cells and organs, for it is when the body is at rest that the dream states begin. The mind does not supplant nor destroy nature, nor does it, under normal conditions, restrict the freedom of the human body. We cannot explore man by dissecting dead bodies, and perforce, we must study the living, conscious man.

There is much group behavior which shows a lack

of adjustment to social conventions, and there are also failures of a similar kind in the mental field. We can apply to groups of men the same criteria that are used to determine whether an individual is adjusted. LeBon, who first called attention to the psychology of the crowd, labored under a social prejudice. He surmised that the crowd thought as a crowd, and explained its behavior from this one angle, because he believed in a collective mind. To him the higher mental faculties and conscious personality became submerged. In this manner, he argued, persons are governed by imitation and suggestion. Crowds will commit acts which the individual would never consider reasonable. The truth is that in crowds and mobs the common impulse is magnified; it is so intensified that the other and superior intuitions are submerged. In considering the societies of the Kingdom of Heaven it is well to hold this truth in mind. In a crowd, where the cohesion is due to a low form of impulsive instinct the true motive of group behavior is disguised, and the projected issue is fictitious. Social control is therefore a form which represses the lower impulse and passion and directs it to corrective ends. The repression when not given orderly outlets creates the mob spirit, and the mob behavior is based on the belief that it is vindicating some ignored universal principle. The crowd is fed on platitudes and catch-words by the oratorical demagogues; in the crowd the individual seeks to throw off the stigma of inferiority, and is led by those who magnify their own abilities and achievements. Gregariousness is natural to man, and it would be well to study more scientifically the motive instincts which impel mob behavior.

We have traced so far some of the aspects of the mind as seen in behavior and dreams. Let us now turn again to the consideration of the main subject. We have found that the mind makes contact with the human body. May we ask why this connection is necessary? The mind makes contact with the body for the same reason that the individual seeks the association of others in society, namely, to satisfy his wants and to develop his empirical knowledge. The body is shaped to the necessities and demands of the mind and fulfils its needs, and it is more perfectly adjusted than is the social system to the individual, for the body never suppresses the impulses and intuitions of the mind. The body carries the desires of the mind into effect and acts regardless whether they are moral or immoral, social or unsocial. The determination of these questions remains always with the mind, and not with the body. There is not one connection of the mind with the body, but many, for the numerous organs, nerve centers, muscles, and cells of the body, in their functioning, illustrate the manifold desires and needs of the mind. The mind requires a complex and harmonious mechanism for its modes of expression. The mind draws not only mechanical activation, but also inspiration from its contact with the brain; it maintains a harmony of relations, and capitalizes the results of the bodily environment.

The mind, which is a superior substance, makes its contacts with the brain on the same principle employed by the nerves, red blood corpuscles, and hormones, in connecting with the organs and muscles. A higher form always proceeds to the lower and not the reverse. The red blood disks attach themselves to the film of the lung chamber and absorb the oxygen. They then proceed to the film of a distant muscle and relinquish the oxygen. It is the superior capillary of the blood, and the superior fiber of the nerve, which penetrates the bone and the muscle. The bone and muscle do not ascend to the nerve and blood. There is no artificial adhesive that connects the mind and body, but the affection of the superior for the uses of the inferior, and hence the cohesion. The individual contributes his services to the social government, for the individual is superior to the government, and the social system is the creation of the individual. Most of the social misconceptions arise when the government is regarded as the superior creation. Government is made for man, not man for the government.

There are innate tendencies in the human mind which determine thought and action, both in the individual and in the collective community. These tendencies are more positive in some individuals than others. The primary tendencies, found in human nature everywhere, furnish a foundation for estimating the history of development in society and its institutions. These primary tendencies have not varied through the literary ages, and they furnish both a basis for comparison and of development among different races and peoples. Only when society in its organization can develop the best in the individual can it be called a success. If it fails in the process it is a sign that wrong principles have been employed, and the demand is for a reconstruction.

Physicists know that the superior powers of the universe are always the invisible forces. Cosmic rays, ether waves, gravitation and light, move rapidly across vast spaces to fixed objects. The force activating any visible object is not from the object, but outside of it. So does mind move within the organs and tissues of the body, its force is seen in the effects produced and in the reactions of the body to the mind. It is the mind that gives meaning to the sensations registered by the body, for it is the mind which converts the objects of matter into symbolic meanings. The human body possesses no such function in itself. James Sully, in his *Outline of Psychology*, says, "The simple act of referring impressions to things or objects in space is the result of a long process of learning by experience."

Man is the acknowledged highest creation in the universe, yet nothing exists in nature which has not some relation to man. Oken says, "The animal kingdom is man disintegrated," which would imply that every animal has some one characteristic that in man is more perfect. The kinship of man to the animal is recognized by the organic sciences, and man's fondness for, and domestication of, animals can be explained from this viewpoint, for in them is something of himself. There is therefore a civilizing force in nature which man acknowledges.

Physical health depends upon the undisturbed working of the cells of the body, disease may grow out of non-coöperative and unbalanced cells which have lost the power of resistance. Just so long as the cells can function in harmony we have health, and this means that the mind must not interfere. However, there are mental disturbances so severe that they have a deterrent effect on the cells of the nerves, and the disorder is apparent in psycho-neurosis. As the state of health and harmony of the body is equally essential to the mind, a diseased body can distress the mind to a point of agony. This effect both ways is due to the fact that the immediate contact of the mind is with the invisible fibers of the cortex of the brain, where sensation is registered. At the cortex the nerve centers are massed, and sensatory pulsations come inward to these fiber ends and contact there with the mind. There are also lesser mind-brain contacts in the cerebellum and medulla oblongata, each of which has a different nerve structure. Sensation comes inward from the skins and bodily films, and mental decisions move outward into muscular action.

The process of the mind is orderly, and from inmosts to outmosts; first, intellect proceeds into thought, then into judgments, and finally to conclusions. The structure of the mind organism is in general divisions comparable to the three distinct divisions of the nerve centers and motors. There are many effects in the process of the mind. The mind has perception because it has will, but perceptions do not proceed into thought until they are stimulated. They are called into action when the mind has something definite in view. These goals may be in the pleasure which the mind derives from harmony, and the insistence of the mind in the preservation of its life. Innate in the mind, which is will and understanding, there is perception of order, of harmonies, and of truths. The mind does not learn the nature of order, harmonies, or truths, except from experience, and this is from the senses of the body.

It may be recognized how important to mind training is the harmony of bodily functions, and why the mind seeks always to maintain the concord and coöperative conjunction. There is no competitive struggle between partnerships, for competition is only between parasitic and predatory types. Success depends upon the sociological factors. It must be admitted that the bodily senses are rather gross, and do not readily absorb the delicate mechanism of the mind. But, it must be remembered that the grosser sensations flow into a corresponding battery of inner and finer sense organs, and that these tone down and refine the outer sensations so that they are more easily acceptable to the mind. This process parallels that of the alimentary canal of the human body, which reduces and refines the grosser parts of food and prepares them for absorption by the blood stream. The mind thus learns from the inner senses, the inner eye and the inner ear, and inner taste and touch, that there is sweetness opposed to bitterness, beauty opposed to ugliness, harmony of sound as opposed to discord, and order as opposed to disturbance. The mind is in constant training from these experiences, therefore a life in this world is absolutely necessary before any one can be introduced into the Spiritual World.

It is in the full measure of one's experiences, and the accumulated knowledge gained therefrom, that the richness of the future life prevails, because the inflow of inmost light and love is into the things which a man has in his mind. A mind that is affirmative to all truth, and negative to error, has the greater possibilities. The mind is constantly making decisions; it either favors or rejects what comes to it from sensation. It learns in this manner what agrees with its harmony, and what disagrees. The character of an individual is determined by the nature of his decisions, and whether they regard solely the ego or the community welfare. Bodily sensation may soothe or pain the mind. When it soothes, the mind is delighted, when it pains, the mind grieves.

The mind, while being trained in this world, clothes itself with a human body in which is sensation, and in this manner the mind is informed on the phenomena of nature. When the human body ceases to function, the mind forms from itself a spiritual body by means of which it comes into a knowledge of the phenomena of the Kingdom of Heaven. The main object which concerns the mind is self-preservation. This is the basic motive in all of its life, the preservation of identity and individuality. It can be known from this that the will of the mind begins with a self-centered motive; it is only from training and experience that the mind learns the value and necessity of the larger community interest. It learns this from the coöperative order of the universe, and its own experience in social government. Everything in nature has an appointed place and duty, and the coöperation maintains order. It can be seen from this why man is related to the universe, for it is part of his education. Animal and plant life not only sustain and feed man, but they are a continual source of information regarding himself. Arthur Thompson has shown that "Man is inseparably linked to the plant kingdom by eternal laws of organic sociology." Man learns the difference between good and evil from his social and world contacts and observations. Fechner, in his book *Ueber die Seelenfrage*, says, "In the cosmic process disharmonies may continue for some time in order to be dissolved into harmony later on. The dissolution of evil is caused by, and consists in, the fact of its antagonisms to the grand order, whereby it stimulates reactions which augment with the evil and finally surpass it in growth, so that the evil is dissolved and finally serves a use. Evil differs from good, in that good serves the purposes of the grand order, but in the end evil is forced to serve the good." In the bio-economic order of evolution the suffering in the world is of a retributive character, and potentially a factor for good. From this it can be seen how important are the lessons derived from man's contact with the world, and how he may unconsciously and unaware imbibe its fundamental teachings. There is a primary truth in the Russian saying that "Nature is man's most exacting school-master."

It is well known that the majority of nerve messages

of the body are not those of sensation, but those concerned with the orderly functioning of the many parts of the body. Also, that the mind is seldom aware of any function of the body, except those major actions which are registered in the cortex of the brain. The mind is concerned far more with its own formations, and with those things which affect its well being. Therefore the major part of the bodily functions are involuntary. Sensation may become passion, and when it does so it is the purpose of the trained mind to regulate and control the passion.

The sense of taste is superior to the sense of touch, because the taste regards the important matter of the food. Life on all levels is faced by the problem of food, and indiscriminate feeding and ineffective assimilation always end in disorders. A body or mind should possess all that is necessary and no more. It is a function of the senses to concern themselves with matters external, and it is the internal matters which occupy the attention of the mind. Atmosphere is very important to the work of the human body, but the mind does not function in this atmosphere, for its realm is superior. The mind has no time-binding or space-binding elements, it can travel around the world in a moment, and can penetrate any natural object; it can even see itself at work.

The bodily senses are closely related to the instincts, for instincts are animal rather than mental functions. The getting of food, acquisitiveness, the expression of physical sex urges, and the sense of amusement in which there is indolence, can be classified as instincts. The interior senses of the mind are concerned with matters which are mostly beyond our present psychological knowledge. The bodily senses are wonderful, which may be known from the structure of the physical

ear, in the minuteness of its parts, and the delicacy of
their arrangement. But far more delicate and sensitive
is the mind's sense of hearing, in which are recorded
vibrations that totally escape the bodily senses. The
mind has taste and hunger, it longs for the food of
knowledge, and it exercises the keenest sense of taste
and discrimination. The character of a mind is known
by the type of food it craves. Knowledge refreshes and
nourishes the mind, it is both drink and food. Some
psychologists speak of this mental craving as curiosity,
which is an error of diagnosis. No mind could be sustained by the elements of curiosity. Curiosity is a dog
sniffing at a bone.

There are as many functions of the mind as there
are functions of the body, and to these the mind adds
many which are unknown to the body. The senses of
the mind are in the pursuit of harmony, just as are
those of the body, but it is an entirely different type of
harmony. What this harmony is like is scarcely known
to man on earth, although he unconsciously experiences
the effects, but he does not know the cause. Physical
speech and its sound is in waves, a type of trembling
which pervades both liquids and solids. Consonants
produce a wave differing from that of the vowels, but
man does not know that consonants correspond to
truths, and vowels are correlated to affections. However, the speech of the mind is felt in ethers which are
beyond and interior to the physical. The physical eye
and optic nerve communicate waves of shade and light
to the mind, but the inner eye of the mind forms images
for itself which in no way resemble the things seen by
the physical eye. Some knowledge of this functioning
can be gained from the cinema process which records
pictures and sounds. The inner eye of the mind is so
sensitive that it can see the objectified pictures in

dreams in which there is no physical light, it can also see spiritual objects by a sense of sight that is called internal vision.

The mind uses the physical eye so that it may form opinions of the objects of the world. It does this from the variety of light and shade, from magnitude, mass, distance, and from motion. But physical pictures are often misleading. The information coming to the mind from the world assists it in forming opinions, and by this knowledge it makes decisions on things seen in the spiritual world. The objects of both worlds take on the same forms and correspond in appearance. In this way the world acts as a teacher to the mind, and helps in its development and education. Therefore every person is born first into the natural world, and from knowledge gained while here, he can be born consciously into the Kingdom of Heaven. One must precede the other, for in all the universe there is a sequence and order.

The human mind may be regarded as a concept-making machine. It continually converts the concrete into the abstract, it recognizes the subtleties and shades of words, and enlarges gradations and relations. Words are verbal concepts and symbols, defining thought, idea and fact. Symbols often are misinterpreted, and therefore words have elusive meanings which entangle definitions. Man deals continually with symbols, the symbol often being the synonym of objects. They have some common ground within which they are interchangeable, but beyond that each has its own special province. Symbols go into the making of systems, and systems again condense into symbols. Minds have a common meeting ground, because the mutual words and ideas have a basis in natural objects that have become familiar to all men. Honesty, truth-

fulness, justice, responsibility, sympathy and charity
are all abstract, for in the processes of the mind a
separation of these elements has been made from all
that does not belong to them. But the mind recognizes
the objective ideas from which they secure their origins. Sensation has taught the mind how to make the
comparisons. And so also with the negatives of pride,
shame, prejudice and rivalry, which are concept definitions springing out of the empirical knowledge in
every-day situations.

Speech and words are part of the equipment of man,
for words represent and symbolize forms, quantities,
qualities and movements. This knowledge assists the
imagination in adjusting itself to the ideas of the mind,
for ideas are likewise symbols and speech. The reason
records and forms judgments from ideas, just as the
eye forms them from objects. The imagination is an
internal sight, far more perfect and sensitive than the
physical eye. The external eye is focused for the moment on a fragment of the object, but the internal eye
sees the complete setting at one time. The internal eye
contacts with all of the cortical fibers, and gets all of
the impressions, and assembles them for the mind.
The mind is in contact with all parts of the human
body, with all of its sensations, but the mind is not a
part of the physical body. Ideas, likewise, are in all of
nature, but they are not part of nature. It is only in
the province of the mind that they can be drawn out
of nature.

The nerve fibers of the brain contract and expand
according to the nature of the inflowing image or object. This systole and diastole movement of the fibers
is inter-related with the idea and image formed in the
mind. The visual image is thus converted and passed
into a mental image or idea of the imagination. These

image-ideas of the imagination are stored in the memory, to be used by the mind when needed to fulfil its thought. The memory and imagination are therefore closely related to the functions of the brain, and all ideas have an object definition. The imagination, in its reactions, preserves all the states produced by the physical senses, but it does not preserve the objects or particulars. It retains only the product of its own reactions, and they can be recalled from the memory in a moment. Therefore any least feeling or state, from childhood to old age, can be revived at any time, and from its qualities the entire picture can be reproduced at will. Every reaction to things seen, heard, or felt, is in the idea, and nothing of which we ever become conscious is lost.

There are times when the imagination, intent upon its reactions, recedes from the cortical fibers of the brain, just as the fibers also harden themselves against the situation in the nerve centers. This act of disengagement is absolutely necessary to both organisms, that of the body and of the mind. There are times when we listen but do not hear, and times when we look but do not observe. So also, while engaged in deep thought or meditation, we are oblivious to all else. The higher purpose momentarily disregards the lower. When a man becomes intelligent and cultured, he regards the small things of life as unimportant, while to the uneducated man these small things are the all of his existence. When absorbed in deep thought, the mind gathers those things which have affinity into a more perfect order, and the discordant things are rejected. It can be seen from this how the mind assimilates and feeds on ideas, and how a similar principle is active in the functions of the alimentary canal and chemical factories of the body.

It is the faculty of perception which permits the mind to know the quality of any object or idea, and the mind is ever intent upon a knowledge of qualities. There is no idea in the memory which has not in some way been stimulated by the imagination, and the imagination gets its food of images from the sensatory communications in the cortical substance of the brain. The imagination is actually the faculty of comprehending all of the things which are obvious to the senses. The imagination is very strong and vivid with children, because they are sensitively engaged with the new objects of nature and with the sense perceptions. But the childhood imagination lacks discrimination, it often confuses fact with fancy, the connection between object and idea is not discerned, and one is taken for the other.

Persons with retarded mentality do not understand the various parts of themselves or their functions. They lack intelligent discrimination and judgment, and when they speak it is from the ideas in the memory. They have not learned how to combine ideas into forms of higher thought. They are easily moved by impulses, and this explains the mass psychology, and the movement of the herd. They prefer the trades in which articles are held in the hands, and all forms of manual labor. Society should therefore always provide hand work, especially where its members are not reflective. The machine age is inclined to disregard this great human need, and much human misery will develop if new inventions deprive these individuals of the employments in which they delight.

Insanity and disease, especially catalepsy, are due to the softening or dissolving of the brain centers. The nerve cells become liquid, something is obstructed in the capillary field and sinuses, and they become sluggish. In all speech there is some mental action, but if the nerve cells through loss of oxygen become liquid, the speech is incoherent and meaningless. The connection between the mind and body has suffered injury, for it is the mind which speaks through the organs of the body. When the image function becomes excited and intoxicated, the toxic condition manifests itself in forms of imbecility and insanity.

In the older psychology, the idea-forming function is called the imagination, and we shall retain that word as more descriptive of the process and less likely to mislead the reader. This idea-forming consciousness is in immediate contact with the sensation centers of the human body, and it picks out the sensatory images and combines them into ideas. In modern psychology, of which there are several schools in combat over terms, the imagination is placed in several departments of the mind, and operations are attributed to it which are confusing. What they assign to the imagination is really the operation of ideation and idealization functions. The imagination is strictly an idea-forming faculty, and it does not fantastically play with the ideas it produces. The ideas are products for the use of the reason, and they are recombined on that higher level.

In considering ideas it is well to know that they have a very intimate biologic affinity; that is, they can be compared to cells in which there are two elements, one essentially formed of affection, and the other strictly intellectual. When the ideas are taken into the rational understanding they are split, very much like chromosomes, and each new division contains its intellectual and its affection element. This is necessarily true because the mind has dual capacities, the mind is a combined will and understanding working in harmony.

The mental life of an individual consists of a large accumulation of ideas which have been produced by the conscious imagination from the sensatory images impinged upon it. These images of the senses do not continue into the memory. They are contiguous and not continuous, for the conscious imagination produces its own forms. It is from this fund of idea material that the mind builds its thought, which forms the basis of its judgments and convictions. The variety of quality in the ideas of the memory is most diverse, because of the particular affection which the individual exercises when it picks the impressions out of the world stream. The imagination manufactures, at the behest of the affection, as many ideas as the mind craves, and they are of such quality as favors and pleases the mind. Every individual has some dominant and controlling love which is continually seeking its delights. It is from the fund of affection-ideas which are agreeable that one person shows ability as a musician or artist, while others are bankers, mechanics, inventors, lawyers, or merchants.

From these descriptions we may learn how the mind makes contact with the human body, how the connection is mutual and beneficial to both, and that it is not severed until the brain centers dissolve. The separation does not take place when the respiration ceases or the heart stops beating, for the connection could be restored so long as the nerve centers are unimpaired. The conscious mind makes contact with the physicochemical and electro-chemical brain, and even at seeming death the organism could be revived if these centers faintly function. When the body finally breaks down, the mind seeks its higher consorts, for the conscious mind knows no death.

Edmund Spenser, in his *Hymne in Honour of Beautie*, says:

> So every Spirit as it is most pure,
>   And hath in it the more of heavenly light,
> So it the fairer body doth procure
>   To habit in, and it more fairly dight
> With cherefull grace, and amiable sight.
>   For of the Soul the body form doth take;
> For Soul is form and doth the body make.

CHAPTER V

THREE PLANES OF THE MIND

My friends inquired
"How did your intellect attain such heights?"
I answered, "By subjecting things to me,
And not myself to them."

Immanuel Ha-Romi.

"WE HAVE done with those hypæthral temples that
were open above to the heavens, but we can have attics
and skylights to them. Minds with skylights, yes—
stop, let us see if we can't get something out of that.
One-story intellects, two-story intellects, three-story
intellects with skylights. All fact-collectors, who have
no aims beyond their facts, are one-story men. Two-
story men compare, reason, generalize, using the labors
of the fact-collectors as well as their own. Three-story
men idealize, imagine, predict; their best illumination
comes from above, through the skylight. There are
minds with large ground-floors, that can store an infinite amount of knowledge . . . without being able
to make much other use of their knowledge." Another
"has two spacious stories; his mind is clear, because
his mental floors are large, and he has room to arrange
his thoughts so that he can get at them—facts below,
principles above, and all in ordered series. Poets are
often narrow below, incapable of clear statement, and
with small power of consecutive reasoning, but full of
light, if sometimes rather bare of furniture, in the
attics." Oliver Wendell Holmes in *The Poet at the
Breakfast Table.*

John Ruskin says, "Your minds are endowed with a

vast number of gifts of totally different uses—limbs of mind as it were, which, if you don't exercise, you cripple."

The human brain is definitely chemical and physico-mechanical, and therefore has no consciousness. Consciousness belongs to the human mind, which is superior to the brain, and therefore may be regarded as spiritual. The nerves do not send verbal messages to the brain centers, for the brain knows nothing of idea or thought. The nerves communicate with the nerve centers by a method of vibration or pulsation, a frequency and variety of wave lengths. It is the mental imagination which observes these wave lengths and variations and interprets them for the mind. It is the mind which makes the determinations and not the brain. The psychic process is not chemical or mechanical, it is spiritual. A radio receiver is mechanical, and may be compared to the human brain, it registers the ether waves; the human being beside the radio interprets the ideas and forms impressions and makes use of them. A radio, no matter how perfect, never learns to think; the human brain, no matter how long used, is incapable of consciousness or thought. The human mind is the conscious, idea-forming organism of man.

In the human mind there are three distinct planes, or fields of operation, each having its given work. The first and lowest of these, the imagination and memory, is external; above this is the understanding and reason, which is intermediary and more perfect; prior to this is the intellect or pure psyche. Some persons use only the imagination and memory, they are undeveloped, lacking in reason and vision, and do not employ the reflective faculty. Other persons use this lower faculty and add to it the reason and understanding, they may or may not be educated, but they have not developed the spiritual faculty of mind. Other persons have developed all three fields of the mind, they are educated and cultured. Culture is the expression of a refined nature, and denotes a high development of the mental and spiritual qualities, which includes the esthetic regard for the rights of others, and reveals itself in the graces of speech and conduct.

How the mind works can be partially understood from the observation of the functions and operations of the human body, for the mind is an organism distinct from the human body, although connected with it in every part. How the contacts between mind and body are made has been explained in the previous chapter, and the process by which the imagination formulates and stores ideas in the memory has also been considered. Above and prior to the imagination and memory is the rational understanding, which has knowledge of the finer implications within each idea, and also a conscious perception of the many differences and contrasts between ideas. The rational understanding is midway between the memory and the pure psyche, and within it are ideas and thoughts both pure and impure, or false and true. The term, pure psyche, is used to define the highest and inmost faculty of mind. In it are the illuminations and the first determinations. If any one prefers to call these three faculties or planes the soul, it is permissible, for definitions and words have peculiar connotations, and when not properly associated they may lead to confusion.

The product of the rational understanding is thought, for it reduces and refines the ideas which it has lifted from the memory, and associates those which harmonize into determinable concepts called thought. Whether the analysis of the rational understanding is orderly or not depends upon the light thrown upon it from the pure psyche, and also by the innate nature of the pure psyche of the individual. There is no thought or wisdom of speech without concordant action of the rational understanding. In studying the subject of the mind we must use the scientific method, for, just as physiologists and chemists know the body from examination and observation of its functions, so the individual can learn the nature and structure of the mind from an inspection of his own mental processes.

It is known that sensations are communicated to the imagination by the frequency of waves in the cortical fibers, and in much the same manner ideas are communicated from the imagination and memory to the rational understanding. By this means the reason has complete knowledge of all the phenomena of nature, for it has command of all that is in the memory, and can lift the memory ideas for instant inspection. To it the past is ever present, and the future may be anticipated from the things of the past. It does not function in time or space, but in the finer spiritual ether. In it are the doubtful and the probable, the true and the false, and by a syncreting and excreting process it arrives at conclusions, and makes determinations. This is the process called thought. It is like an eye which sees light and shadows, and it focuses on the picture it wants. These pictures are coördinated and kept in series.

The faculty of rational understanding is prior to the imagination and senses. It is not acquired from them—it is embryonic in the child at birth, and never changes its form. Every faculty of the mind has both an internal and an external. The external faculty of the rational understanding can be developed and trained, but not so with the internal faculty. In its functioning the rational understanding disposes and puts in order all of the ideas gathered for it by the imagination, otherwise it could form no conclusions of thought. There can be arguments by men as to the nature and proper use of truth, but no argument as to truth itself, for its quality is not dependent upon argument or decisions. Truth is the form in which pure love expresses itself in the mind, and love accepts the truth which agrees with it. Men may disagree in their opinions and ideas concerning the laws of nature, but whatever view they hold does not change the action of those laws. It is according to the nature of a man's love whether he regards nature as hostile or as favorable; he may learn from nature, or he may discredit its teaching. Planets and solar systems moved in their allotted orbits long before men were aware of movement or orbit. Truth itself is eternal, but it is modified and colored by the individual thought and aspect.

The words used in speech are really symbols and images of ideas, but the operating reason does not heed the words, it creates forms more like parables and similitudes. What is meant by this can sometimes be recognized in the dream states, which are throw-offs from the rational mind at the time when the senses are dormant and the imagination inactive. There can be no thought where the imagination has not produced the idea-forms, for the imagination is the reproduced memory of things seen, felt, and heard. From this fund of idea-forms the thought can develop new ideas, and it does this by rearranging the ideas received from the memory, thus creating new images and similitudes suggested by the concordant relationships. The rational understanding has intuition and perception of many forms which escape the imagination. It is by means of these new creations that forms

and ideas are present in dreams, wholly unlike anything the person has seen or known. The ideas of the
imagination are obtained from the sensory fibers; the
ideas of the thought are geometric figures far beyond
the sensory ideas. When the serious and concentrated
thought reduces its own ideas into perceptible forms
they are held and stored by the rational mind.

By the processes of deduction, analysis, and refinement, the rational understanding gains practice and
perfection. Unless ideas are classified and grouped, no
conclusions would follow thought. The elaborated idea-
forms become the individual's fund of knowledge, upon
which the rational understanding continually draws
while in meditation, and in urgent need. Men have this
knowledge in different degrees, in some the knowledge
is confined to their particular vocation, in others there
is a broad and comprehensive fund of knowledge. Men
search for and use the knowledges which appeal to
their individual affections and further their interests.

Strange as it may seem, genius is often peculiarly
the perfection of the imagination and the sensories.
We frequently attribute genius to men who simply
have originated a method of overcoming physical disturbances and mental intrusions. These men have taken
advantage of circumstances and by mental alertness
have arrived at conclusions ahead of others. The occasion often makes the man, and this combined with
public opinion produces an illusion of genius. Men very
strong in character have often been defeated by circumstances within their immediate environment. To
be very frank, the human race has produced no perfect
men. Some men have risen to prominence because the
average ability of mankind is very deficiently expressed.
The majority of mankind are easily given to routine,
suspicious of innovations, and timid of adventure.

When any individual seeks seriously the undiscovered, insists on seeing things other than they seemed before, and then works for a reconstruction, he makes a high mark of ability. Few men ever achieve a full rounded character, and the life of no seemingly great man will bear close inspection without revealing flaws of character. The very nature of our mental education seems to forbid originality and character of a superior order among the masses.

John Stuart Mill said, "History shows that great economic and social forces flow like a tide over communities only half-conscious of that which is befalling them. Wise statesmen observe what is likely to come and attempt to shape institutions and mold men's thoughts to purposes in accordance with the change that is silently moving toward them."

Whatever we have learned as a race has come out of the coöperative effort, and not from individual and detached struggle, freed from personal interests. It is from the group effort that man has revolutionized his environment and molded circumstances. He has multiplied the comforts and conveniences, but has not increased morality or developed spirituality, for human conduct and behavior are still medievalistic and pagan. Even to-day, our knowledge of the higher aims and possibilities of society is merely academic. The caliber of the mass mind can be seen in the social organizations, political governments, and business affairs of the day, and these define its quality. The level of social understanding is rather low, and if correctives are to be applied, the beginning must be in the will and mind of individuals. Human affairs are in themselves more intricate and perplexing than molecules and chromosomes—they are in the mind of man.

Dr. A. Meikeljohn has often said that "education

as now practiced cannot go on successfully without some considerable change in the social order, a change approaching a social revolution." The modern need is not for new scientific achievements, but for ethical and spiritual understanding of Life's verities; not moral knowledge alone, but methods for the practice of spiritual ideas in the common affairs of men. Much of the education as now conceived is a preparation for the same kind of citizenship which has failed in the past to remove the shocking hazards and crying injustices which torment the present social and political régime. Charles P. Steinmetz, the electrical engineer, was asked, "What line of research will have the greatest development during the next fifty years?" His reply was, "I think the greatest discoveries will be made along spiritual lines. History clearly teaches that spiritual forces have been the greatest power in the development of men and nations. Yet we have been merely playing with them, and have never seriously studied them as we have the physical forces. Some day people will learn that material things do not bring happiness, and are of little use in making men and women creative and powerful. Then the scientists of the world will turn their laboratories over to the study of God and prayer, which as yet have hardly been touched. When this day comes, the world will see more advancement in one generation than it has witnessed in the past four."

Youth's mentality is often immature and impatient, for calm judgment belongs to the experiences of many years. Age has this disadvantage, it often holds the traditional prejudices and misconceptions which atrophy and arrest mental growth. There must be a genuine understanding of all conditions, and this is made possible by exercise of the inner perception and sensation of the human reason. When intuition is active, the trained reason can know instantly whether a proposition is true or false. The faculty of meditation is also capable of abuse; if it is centered on one set of ideas persistently there may arise fantasies and hallucinations. Psychiatrists trace many forms of psychosis to the patient's continual fixed thought on single ideas connected with the self-interest and ego. Dwelling mentally on single ideas magnifies their importance, destroys orderly relationships between ideas, and engenders fear; the fear may easily become an obsession that gets beyond control. These distorted image-forms born of an excited imagination move wildly in dream and waking states, and defy normal interpretation.

The rational understanding, by means of thought, forms analytical and rational equations after having arrived at conclusions, but these are not ultimated in act and deed unless sent through the will. The will does not force them into action unless there is in the conceived goal a desired end. It is evident that the matured mind can be engaged in constructive thought when the individual develops his rational understanding. By the type of thinking and feeling which he exercises, a man creates his own world; if his thoughts are vague and inconclusive, his world will be of the same pattern. Often the desires are self-centered, and regard his personal advantage and convenience, if so, his world will be one of exploitation, and his philosophy one of greed and pride. The structure of the human mind is such that it contains all of the potential resources essential to satisfaction; it has also within itself the command of a technique which would make the world more enjoyable, not only to the individual, but to all others. Nature has silently furnished abundant materials, she has laid them in the path of man, but she has left no instructions on their proper use. Man must somehow not only find himself, but he is compelled to invent an art which will make the world of use to him. He must write his own books, be his own school-master, invent his own tools, and suffer his own mistakes.

When in the dim beginning of the years,
    God mixed in man the raptures and the tears
And scattered through his brain the starry stuff,
    He said, Behold! Yet this is not enough,
For I must test his spirit to make sure
    That he can dare the Vision and endure.

I will withdraw my face,
    Veil Me in shadow for a certain space,
Leaving behind Me only a broken clue—
    A crevice, where the glory glimmers thru,
Some whisper from the sky,
    Some footprint on the road, to track Me by.

I will leave man to make the fateful guess,
    Will leave him torn between the No and Yes,
Leave him unresting until he rests in Me,
    Drawn upward by the choice that makes him free—
Leave him in tragic loneliness to choose,
    With all in life to win, or all to lose.

Children require education and protection, for there are few ideas and no equations in infancy, and therefore no serious thought-forms. Childhood is taxed heavily by the demands of physical growth; at the same time the imagination is building rapidly, shaping its images from the stream of sensory pulsations. Youth is imitative, it attempts to resent imaginary wrongs, it labors under an intense desire to reconstruct its world, and conform it to the impulsive pattern. The undeveloped rational mind is unable to function in or-

derly manner for there are not sufficient idea-forms
upon which the mind can operate, or from which
healthy conclusions can be drawn. It is difficult to say
at what age the rational mind begins to function;
some adults are mentally immature. It is true that at a
very early age we have all of the material from which
character is produced, but the arrangement of the elements is a life-long process.

There are wise provisions in the mental development
of an individual, for the lower plane of the mind is
absorbing material and arranging it before the higher
faculties begin to operate. The lower the operating
faculty the less efficient is the mental apprehension, but
each plane of the mind is competent to express itself
in words and deeds. It is possible, for instance, to speak
and act solely from the imagination and memory faculty, and to continue to do so through life; it is equally
true that the same may be done from the lower faculty
and with the added rational understanding; or, all
three planes may be active, which would include that
of the pure intellect. When these facts are taken into
consideration they will explain the great variety of
mental and emotional activities and conditions prevailing in the world. In the lower mental states errors and
fallacies are more abundant. There is a confusion of
images and ideas because the higher faculties do not
operate and are not trained to the refinement and separation of ideas. In the lower mentalities the impulses
are ungoverned, and the habit of imitation is acquired
as a self-defense method. These minds reverence authority and repeat the words and gestures of those
whom they admire.

The rational understanding has a life independent
of all which is below it. It receives this life from the
pure intellect, and although it may not be known con-

sciously by the individual or even consulted, the rational has an awareness of every change taking place in the imagination, the memory and the sensories. This awareness belongs to it from the first breathings of the infant, for by means of the contact the physical life is involuntarily maintained. It may be seen that the reasoning faculty is essential to life, although the person may not use it for his own advancement mentally. It maintains an indirect contact and control of the body, and it can restore harmony and order when the unleashed will might have caused havoc and ruin. The reason, by the indirect connection, preserves and guides all of the involuntary actions of the human body. The physical body has no consciousness of its own, no sense of direction, or ultimate purpose; the determinations come from within the rational mind. By the functioning power of the rational faculty, as a means, the pure intellect is attentive to all of the operations of the body, and in all consciousness, but it does not communicate knowledge of its presence. The pure intellect, when not employed by the individual consciously, permits the reason to act in its own way in the government of the body. It allows the rational mind and the human body to suffer the misdeeds and penalties of their own disorders. The pure intellect preserves its own integrity, and by its independence of the lower organs it retains a freedom of choice between order and disorder, and between harmony and discord.

It may be seen that it is with the individual whether he employs the pure intellect, for it is a hidden and secret power ready at his command, but it will not be consciously active unless the motive and interests of the person are of a spiritual nature. It cannot be degraded in its service, but it gives to a man of spiritual insight a tremendous stimulus and power. It grants him a perspective of life as a whole, and initiates him into the eternal secrets of plan and purpose in life. The man who will seriously engage the whole of his mind finds contentment and joy in all active and unselfish service. Mentally he can rise above all of the disturbances and turmoils of the world and work in partnership of kindred souls for great and worthy ends. His will is fashioned to a guidance and leadership which come from within, and what he does is not strictly from himself, but contains purposes of which he is but a part. This feeling of comradeship with great minds is the most noteworthy achievement of life, for these men hold the psychic world in balance, and the destiny of races and governments rests finally upon them. They are not politicians, their names may not be known to the public, they are the seers and prophets who stand upon the mountain peaks of humanity, and their thought is centered upon a light which the masses never see.

The rational understanding, by means of thought, makes its own decisions and forms its conclusions. It contemplates the ideas which the imagination has prepared in the light that comes from the pure intellect, for the rational occupies a middle ground, and if there were no ideas and no light, it could not function. There are persons who jump from one idea to another, seemingly without coherent connection. This is caused by an excited imagination which throws ideas into the mind and then hastily withdraws them. The fluctuation and alternation is evidence of an incomplete process of the mind, for the rational mind is not operating as it should. The rational mind must be trained to assemble and hold its thought against assault, by lifting it to higher levels. Superficial thinking is the opposite of meditative thought, and there is a common weakness to both styles which becomes apparent when they persist.

Every individual has unrealized capacities and unused resources. It is difficult to re-assess our own surroundings and to see our own position, because they are so much a part of ourselves. This ability of detachment is within us if we learn how to exercise it. We must know historically how conditions came to exist, and we must have something more perfect as a comparison. If a man will withdraw into his own mind and evaluate his own mental processes, keeping in thought the fundamental principles of action, he can arrive at safe and sane conclusions. In all of the universe, as well as within himself, every form has its relation to a prior and superior form, the lower presents its own given phenomena which are the result of its own peculiar reactions. Man may be regarded as of a dual nature, in which the human body is the lower and visible, and the mind is the higher and invisible. There is a firmly established partnership between the two, which is not dissolved except at the point of death in the body.

The higher and more perfect organism of the mind continues its existence after parting from the body, for the mind from experience is adapted to the succeeding environment of the spiritual world and the Kingdom of Heaven. When the contact with the physical body is broken, the organism of the mind by its inherent nature clothes itself with a spiritual form, and by means of it becomes fully conscious of the higher and superior plans and purposes. What takes place in the changed form is simply a repetition of the process of natural birth, for by a similar adaptation the body of the infant man came forth from the womb and accommodated itself to the conditions and environment of this world. The physical birth was into a time-limited world and required nine months to mature sufficiently for its first venture into this world. The spiritual birth has no time-space boundaries, for the human mind is already conscious of itself, and the birth into the other world is immediate. There are no miracles or contradictions in the fundamental principles of life and action, although our lack of understanding may lead us astray in assuming that spirit and flesh are both material. The person who does not believe in life after death has not by that unbelief annihilated himself. He will discover his continued life in due course, and no doubt rejoice in the survival. Whether we agree or not, we are indissolubly bound together as fellow creatures, and it is well to make the most of our privileges and opportunities. There will never be lacking a supply of mystery, for our minds follow very carefully the trodden paths. Mystery is part of life's anticipations, and we simply cannot explain everything in scientific and rational terms. The mysteries of the past ages have dissolved and disappeared in the light of modern knowledge, and the mysteries of today will follow in their time the same order of clarification.

To view life in a large way, let us think of the external nature of man as animal, for it has its own physical limits above which it cannot rise; let us then admit that the higher faculties of man are of the angelic nature, for they are eternal and persistent. It is this thought which inspires poets and artists, and it will bring comfort and peace to any person who will seriously entertain it. This does not mean that the animal can be indulged and at the same time the angel be preserved. Every horse must be bridled and saddled before it can be ridden; so must the animal nature be curbed and controlled into right paths. It may be necessary at times for the angel, with drawn sword, to block the way lest the false Balaam and his ass mislead us.

Charles Edward Russell has said, "To make money is nothing, most of the money makers I have known led lives flatter than a stove-lid. To get office or distinction is nothing; of the men that fifty years ago had all the limelight, hardly one still clings by so much as a shred to the human memory. The one purpose that seems to have sanity or actual reward is to keep step, however stumbling, however far in the rear, with the vast, silent, often mysterious, sometimes scarcely discernible, processes that are slowly transforming the world from a wolf's den to a place where man can know some peace, some contentment, some joy of living, some sense of the inexhaustible beauties of the universe in which he has been placed."

While in this world we are known to other men from our physical appearance, tone of voice, and manner of acting. Upon better and fuller acquaintance they know our states of mind, interests, and dispositions, and from these they are drawn to us in friendships, or repelled and separated. Our conduct and behavior are the expression of our minds and our affections, and establish our reputation. Our basis of association is not resting on physical appearances, but upon the concordance of mutual interests, ideas, and thoughts. There is in all friendships, however, some illusion and concealed reserve, for the individual's inmost nature is rarely known to himself and never to others. It is the holiest of holies where the cherubim with outstretched wings stand guard over the ark of life.

The human mind is composed of will and understanding, and it is by means of these two faculties or forces that experience has meaning, and they permit man to escape from the dull routine of the lower creatures. The understanding registers what a man does with his will. The will and understanding are two distinct substances and capacities, intimately related, yet each with its definite functions; in no thought, idea, word or gesture, are they ever separated or absent. There are occasions when the understanding refuses to concur, when the will insists on ultimating its desires, but the will is so powerful that it can compel coöperation. Heraclitus has said, "Eyes and ears make bad witnesses for a barbarous soul." There is often an inner conflict between reason and desire; understanding may visualize some creative ideal which requires sacrifice of self, but the insistence of the will may convert it to selfish ends. Seneca may have had something of this in mind when he said of Diogenes, "We have all failed, and will continue to do so until overtaken by gray-bearded age. The evil cause does not lie outside of us; it strives in our inward soul. The body of man is a mere instrument, and victim of the spirit. The soul drives toward the goal from whence it came." It is true that no mind is capable of sustained or long flight, for its destination is controlled by the nature and desire of the individual emotions.

The will of man has various modes of expression: first, love, which is an intense emotion of many and varied types; second, affection, a deep feeling going out to persons and things; third, attraction, which is often promoted by mutual understandings; fourth, liking, which is a milder form of feeling directed to things that satisfy desire; fifth, emotion, which is a tremor or internal sensation; sixth, desire, which may be a fancy, appetite, disposition, or lively interest. The inmost love of any person is individual, it is unlike that of any other; it operates on the spiritual plane, and it is the secret power-house of man's motives, inclinations, and consequent action. It is in the will that man finds his own center; it provides him an escape from being thrown on a dizzy mechanism which demands a succession of external adjustments. The will may have for its ends either the pure or the impure; the one controlling force upon it is the trained understanding, the rule of reason, and by this means an equilibrium can be maintained over the impure. In the mind there is always an immediacy of the eternal, and in its pursuit of natural and spiritual truth the understanding can enlist the power of the will, and thus attain elements that establish harmonies. The function of the understanding is to discover a technique by which the will can express itself in orderly and constructive ways. Just as the sculptor wields a crude hulk of clay, and by a few swift and deft strokes the master-hand shapes it into a work of art, so the intelligence can guide the affection and create the beautiful. Primitive people are emotional and not intellectual, therefore they are not creative.

All systems and methods of education are directed to the training of the understanding, and it is the expectation of educators that the will may concur in the effort. It is for this reason that the interest of the pupil must be sustained, for interest is indicative of affection. Education provides outlets as an escape from consuming desires that are blind and staggering. In childhood the will is restrained, for if suddenly given power to create or produce, the value of the product would be questionable. What would it create? At birth the will is the only active force of the infant, because the will is its life, but the infant has nothing of understanding; it requires time, experience, and many types of fact and truth to train the understanding. No child need be taught to love, but it must be shown how to think. The relationship of the will and the understanding may be compared to a marriage, in which the understanding is the male factor, and the will the female factor. The will proceeds to its creative goal by means of intuitions and desires; the understanding arrives at its conclusions by a method of reasoning. The understanding sees, but the will feels. It need not be assumed that the will is always perverse, for this is not true, there is an inherent sense of love toward the neighbor in many men. Lawyers know that in pleading with a jury they can rest assured that the majority have a keen sense of justice and of right action, and this appeal is frequently awarded. If the will is wantonly inclined the understanding must protect and secrete its truths and thus prevent their violation.

The will, in its various expressed forms, is active on all three levels of the mind; it has both an internal and external form, of which the external is more easily misled. When the will is overstimulated or indulged, it leads to insanities and crime. The process of the pure intellect is always through the will to the understanding and not the reverse. Unless the will of man is devoted to the higher and idealistic ends the pure intellect cannot be employed. The will is heated by its loves, but the understanding is made active by light. The will cannot be trained, but it may be controlled and refined so that it prefers that which is for the good of all. The will produces motives and emotions, the understanding presents and observes sensations. Any idea which comes into the thought does not proceed to the act and deed unless it first comes to the will. The will generates power. It is by the function of the will that a man can give out and receive love; the function of the understanding creates and gives out thought. The understanding has no love of its own. It is devoted to discovery and exploration for the sake of truth, and the will uses these discoveries and directs them to definite ends.

The quality of an individual is to be known primarily by what he loves and wills. It is therefore exceedingly difficult to classify men and place them in observable categories because the inmost love and will are concealed from observation. The rational mind instructs the will what it ought to love, what to wish, and what to avoid. There is frequently a conflict between them which destroys the peace of mind, for the will runs in the habit grooves and declines to be coerced by the reason. Force of habit is really the dominating will seeking easy outlets. The will often desires to expand its experiences, and may then act with or without consent of the reason. Freedom of rational choice is lost when the will becomes imperialistic, because obedience to reason's dictates is ignored and violated. The will is so powerful that it can regard a future or possible event and bring it to pass, and either good or harm may ensue to the individual. The will must not be confused with love, for the will has the capacity to love or to hate; it is the *receptorium* of spiritual heat and it is the living conatus in man. It may be seen from this that the office of the understanding is to purify and correct the will.

These are the elemental facts concerning the nature and structure of the human mind, and they explain why there is such a great variety in human nature, and in individual dispositions, for there are no two inclinations or interests which are exactly similar. Some persons desire to be wise, others strive to be useful, others wish to be honorable in all affairs, and again others are inclined to gratify the craving for pleasure and idleness. Some men affect to be good for the sake of their reputation, who if uncontrolled would be most evil. Thus the restraining effect of social customs and public opinion is civilizing. In this world we often show the unlovely side of our natures, and it is therefore necessary that man should be freed of his errors and gradually brought into an order of social behavior and understanding. In retarded and abridged mental states the unnatural desires become the driving force, and there is therefore a demand for wise and careful mental training.

It is doubtful whether any one is wilfully or consciously evil and unsocial. Probably he is ignorant and undeveloped, or has a twisted philosophy of life. It is claimed for Judas Iscariot that by betraying Jesus he hoped for the overthrow of the Jewish rulers. Because motives are so concealed in this world there is all the more reason why the final showdown should come in the next world, and an opportunity granted for the working out of the best in the individual.

Locke, in his treatise on *The Human Understanding*, says, "I do not doubt but that in the state and present constitution of our nature, human knowledge may be carried far beyond any point thus far attained, if men will undertake sincerely and with entire mental freedom to perfect the means of discovering the truth with the same application which they employ in coloring and maintaining a falsity, in defending a system on which they are declared partisans, or certain interests in which they are engaged. There is a science of sciences, which is connate in the soul."

Why do we do the things, and engage in the interests which occupy so much of our life? When the composer, Bach, was asked why he composed music, his brief reply was, "For the love of God, and a pleasant occupation."

An ancient parchment recently discovered in Egypt is said to contain one of the teachings of Jesus the Christ. It reads: "Ye ask who are those that draw us to the kingdom, if the kingdom is in heaven? The fowls of the air, and all the beasts that are under the earth or upon the earth, and fishes of the sea, these are they which draw you; and the kingdom of heaven is within you, and whosoever shall know himself shall find it. Strive therefore, to know yourselves, and ye shall be aware that ye are the sons of the Almighty Father; and ye shall know that ye are in the city of God, and ye are the city."

It is only the human mind that can see the relationship between the two worlds, matter and spirit; every human act points to something mental and spiritual.

> Back of the beating hammer
>   By which the steel is wrought,
> Back of the workshop's clamor
>   The seeker may find the Thought,
> The Thought that is ever master
>   Of iron and steam and steel,
> That rises above disaster
>   And tramples it under heel!
>
> The drudge may fret and tinker
>   Or labor with dusty blows,
> But back of him stands the Thinker,
>   The clear-eyed man who knows;
> For into each plow or sabre,
>   Each piece and part and whole,
> Must go the Brains of labor,
>   Which gives the work a soul.

There is the eye which scans them
  Watching through stress and strain,
There is the Mind which plans them—
  Back of the brawn, the Brain.

Yes, back of them stands the Schemer,
  The Thinker who drives things through;
Back of the job—the Dreamer
  Who's making the dream come true.

CHAPTER VI

THE FUNCTIONS OF THE HUMAN BODY

Man is all symmetry;
Full of proportions, one limb to another,
    And to all the world besides.
    Each part may call the farthest, brother;
For head with foot hath private amity,
    And both with moons and tides.

Nothing hath got so far
But man hath caught and kept it as his prey;
    His eyes dismount the highest star,
    He is, in little, all the sphere.
Herbs gladly cure our flesh, because that they
    Find their acquaintance there.

For us the winds do blow,
The earth doth rest, heaven move, and fountains flow.
    Nothing we see but means our good,
    As our delight, or as our treasure;
The whole is either our cupboard of food;
    Or cabinet of pleasure.

The stars have us to bed;
Night draws the curtain, which the sun withdraws;
    Music and light attend our head.
    All things unto our flesh are kind
In their descent and being; to our mind
    In their ascent and cause.

More servants wait on man
Than he'll take notice of. In every path

He treads down that which doth befriend him,
When sickness makes him pale and wan.
O! mighty love! Man is one world, and hath
Another to attend him.

NEW knowledge of man's origin and nature is now contributed by biology, chemistry, anthropology, and psychology. But let us remind ourselves that while science has achieved many things it does not cover the entire field of man's activities; rather, the important and more involved functions escape the domain of scientific investigation. There is much in the secretion of the human body that remains unknown. In the realm of spirit, morals, motives, loves and emotions, and the intuitive spiritual urges elude the probing test-tube of the laboratory. Men have always escaped the here and now, for the inner spirit cannot be chained or held in space-time cells; its romantic longings and spiritual cravings have climbed to worlds more sweetly and gracefully molded to its fancies.

The human body is a completely organized society of living microscopic units. It is the most highly evolved organism coming within the knowledge of man, and is therefore worthy of the most serious study. For two thousand years learned men have dissected and analyzed the body in the effort to disclose its secrets. Herbert Spencer, in the year 1850, began a study of the ideal form of government and he hoped that biology might furnish an example. He therefore searched the human body as a pattern for the successful society and studied its rules of government, and it was not long before he finally concluded that no existing or previous form of human society ever approached the perfection of the bodily organism.

To fully describe the operations and processes of the human body would require a large Latin vocabulary, and an understanding of mechanical engineering and many of the sciences. There are interesting elementary facts which every one should know concerning the body as a whole, for it is the unit of operation which is vital, and not the segmentary functions or isolated parts. In an attempt to make this summary, let us learn of the several systems and their joint operations.

The Alimentary Canal

The body must obtain food, and the metabolism in building life substances out of non-living matter is an indispensable law of self-preservation. This process begins in the alimentary canal, which is some twenty-eight feet in length, and links up with important chemical factories of the body. It is a transportation system in which the traffic flows in only one direction, that is, from the mouth inward and downward. Food is a type of fuel, and has a caloric content as well as nourishing properties; the heat units in food have been mathematically estimated. The body, unlike any mechanical engine, maintains a uniform internal temperature regardless of the winter or summer conditions prevailing on the outside of the body. Should the body temperature abnormally increase, say to 105° F., the central nerve system would be seriously impaired. To prevent undue drain of heat from the body, there are layers of fat spread under the skin, for the skin plays an important part in both evaporation and conservation. To overcome the drain of moisture in summer, the body signals for a new supply of liquids, and the call-bell is known to us by the sensation of thirst.

To make the food palatable it must be flavored, for the food of man is composed of raw materials which have not been predigested. The raw food demands an elaborate system of digestion, for it consists of many varieties, and when food is needed the signal comes to us by means of the alarm-clock called hunger. The pangs of hunger originate at the nerve cells within the muscles of the stomach. Thirst begins at the throat muscles and the cry is taken up by the nerves. The demand for pure air, from which oxygen is to be extracted, causes the medullary nerve centers to contract the muscles of respiration. In all instances the distress signals arise in the muscles.

By delicate and sensitive chemical reactions, the lips first sample the food, and after the teeth have broken apart the harder parts, the tongue takes more samples, and the blood stream begins to absorb the finer essences. Let us not forget the nose, for the sensitive smell has already approved the incoming supply of food. Passing these three tests, should the tongue disagree, the mouth spits out the food if it proves too hot or unwholesome. Appetite also has part in deciding what food shall enter; and the nerves at the base of the teeth send out notice that food is on the way. Thus the body has ample protection in its fuel consumption.

After these tests the fuel passes from one chemical factory to another, where it is separated, sorted, and directed to the consumers. It is in the partnership of these organs that the body finds the solution of its problems. The chamber of the stomach, into which the food passes, is not rigid but contracts and expands as required: this is effected by the two layers of muscles in the walls of the stomach. All along the line of transportation the local nerve cells not only keep in touch with the operations, but they are aware of the temperatures.

Let us go back to the beginning and note some of

the features of the work. We find that the lower teeth press the food against the upper teeth, and that this is done by the muscles of the jaw. Teeth come to us full size, they do not grow larger. When the child mouth enlarges, the baby teeth drop out, and a new set is provided. Thus does the body care for its sustenance. There are three pairs of salivary glands in the mouth. These open and pour out a fluid, saliva, which acts as a solvent; even the sight or smell of food will open them. A dog's mouth waters when he sees meat. This saliva is often charged heavily with mineral salts and a deposit of tartar forms inside the lower teeth.

The food does not pass along by gravity, but by a system of automatic control induced by the pressure of the coördinated muscular walls. The dissolved food waits for the gates to open, and pressure is given as the gates close behind it. This operation is something like that of gates or locks in a ship canal. Every mouthful of food is in contact with millions of spindles, actively set in motion, and by the breaking process new elements are exposed in the chyme. All of the time the capillaries and arteries are working in conjunction with the muscles, and the system very nicely takes care of the load. From the moment food leaves the mouth it requires some eight seconds to reach the stomach.

The stomach is a factory which produces chyme, a semi-digested fuel in liquid form, the stomach having poured quantities of gastric juice into the contents. The gastric juice has two effects, it stimulates and it prevents fermentation of the food. It should be noted that the state of the mind has an immediate influence on the action of the stomach and intestines. Therefore, pleasant conversation and laughter at the table are helpful, and low spirits or loneliness are to be avoided. In all of the laboratories and functions there is some refuse, which by means of convenient sluice-gates is carried to other organs for processing. The stomach does not digest sugar, starches, or fats, for these go to other chemical factories. The stomach primarily prepares the nitrogen-carrying elements, the vegetable matter and their vitamines. The stomach has a pulse beat of its own, and this is true of every bodily laboratory along the canal. Each has a factory hum, a tune and a rhythm. Also, along the line of digestion, the blood has been active in absorbing the finer and subtle essences, so that nothing valuable to the body is lost.

The stomach passes the chyme to the duodenum and the intestines in small quantities, where it is to be converted into finished products ready to be consumed in the tissues of the body. We may think of the intestines as a corridor or channel some twenty feet in length, where the larger molecules are separated and torn apart; it is here that the ferments begin their work, for trypsin, an active ferment, is injected into the starches and sugars. Another ferment called lipase is carried in by the blood cells. It is an enzyme which attacks and splits open the fats. The chemical factory which produces enzymes and ferments is called the pancreas. The common name is sweetbreads. These enzymes and hormones are wonderful products, very small, and when finished are sent in packages, like the parcel-post system, to specified points in the body, and they are not interfered with or opened until they reach their destination. Complete utilization of food is seldom possible, for most persons eat more than is required. This often impairs the organs of digestion, rendering them incapable of complete absorption. The body takes only what it needs.

The liver is considered to be the greatest chemical factory of the body. It receives all of its material from the blood circulating along the outside of the alimentary canal. These are the essences which the blood stream has been collecting from the digestive canal. The work of the liver is to convert these substances into food and fuel for the tissues of the body. It is a combined laboratory and storehouse, for it holds the carbohydrate product called glycogen, which is a white, mealy compound, in reserve until orders are received from the consumers. When the order comes in, the glycogen is reconverted into blood-sugar before it is sent on its way. There is also a by-product extracted by the liver, a colorless compound called urea, which is sent direct to the kidneys for processing. Some other by-products in small quantities are sent to the gallbladder. Of the uses of this organ little is known. It seems to attract the contaminated and vitiated blood and subject it to a whirling process. The spleen is another laboratory in which the blood cells are elaborated and old cells broken down. There pass into it compounds of pure and impure blood, and these are manipulated and separated, the waste rejected, and the salvage sent back into the blood stream.

After this consideration of the factories let us go again to the main line of the alimentary canal, for these laboratories are set apart so that they may work undisturbed. We have noted that the digestive tract of the intestines has sent many extracts to the laboratories. After everything has been done to take the soluble substances from the food, the residue is sent to the large bowel, where an entirely new process begins. It may be said again that science is far from a complete knowledge of the mechanics of the human body, and the work of the large bowel is still shrouded in uncertainty. In poetic language the bowels are regarded as the seat of tender and sympathetic emotions.

This idea arises from the feeling of muscular actions which are evidenced in given states of mind, for the mind is keenly influenced and also exerts an influence on the chemical action and organs of the body.

The new process in the large bowel is that of the introduced bacteria, which are microscopic cells of various sizes and shapes, which feed on the cast-off refuse. When furnished this nutriment, they synthesize the material of their own bodies, they grow fat and divide, and this process continues so long as temperature and food are agreeable. They perform many useful tasks, but may also, if over-multiplied, cause disorders and disease. The length of their life depends upon the power of synthesis. Why are they employed by the body? It seems that the operations of the intestines would become too exhaustive if the work on the food were further continued, and the body cells therefore call in outside helpers. They are the cheap laborers. They consume no bodily energy for they live on the refuse and waste. It is well known that men have invented mechanical processes to extract oils and liquid compounds from the garbage heaps of large cities, and this is a type which the human body has contrived in elaborating cheap machinery for similar work in the large bowel. Ferments in the intestines have naturally created gases, and these gases and fumes are now reduced to liquids by the bacteria. The alimentary canal, having drawn off all of the substances of food and drink which it requires, then throws out the unused excess.

The Bones of the Body

The human body is held in shape by the bones, formed of mineral salts. Lifeless as the bones appear, they present many features of interest, and perform an unusual service. In the infant the bones are soft, and of a cartilaginous nature, for it requires twenty years to properly build and solidify them. The two hundred bones of the body turn freely and wonderfully on fixed fulcrums, imparting pressure from a source of power to resistance. Bone is built mostly from the inside, where millions of corpuscles, called bone builders, are at work. They not only construct, but, as the individual grows older, they constantly lengthen, alter and rebuild the periosteum in most marvelous ways. All of this reconstruction must go on without any interference with the activities of the body, day or night. It is marvelous how these workers construct the forms, especially at the ages when the body is growing rapidly. To get some idea of their numbers, it has been estimated that there are two million bone builders in the thigh-bone of a child. The workers not only build, but at times they tear down before reconstructing. Broken and fractured bones require adjustment, the destructive microbes not allowed to gather, and then the workers begin when the blood circulation is restored. If there are any germs, the chemistry of the body drugs them and forces them to good work. It takes about six weeks for the bone repair to be completed, and then the connection is stronger than it was previously. Thus the body effects its own cure, the physician merely giving the millions of workers the freedom of operation.

The general outline of the skeletal frame is too well known, even to the school child, to require a description here. At the ends of each bone we find a softer, elastic substance called cartilage, which contains no blood vessels, and the firmer building goes forward in it. The workers in the cartilage sacrifice their lives by dissolving into lubricants, so that the joints may move noiselessly and freely. How necessary this movement is may be understood when we are told that fifty joint bearings must be lubricated at each step we take. There are some 230 joints in the human body, and eighty-four of them move with each breath taken into the lungs. The soft cartilage serves as a buffer, reducing the effect of a jolt, as in jumping. The cells also drain the excess lubricating fluid and then store it for future use, by returning it to the blood stream. In this manner nothing useful is lost.

The age of the individual does not concern the cells, for they are always alert and work incessantly. The weight of the bones has been estimated at one-fourth of that of the whole body. It may be imagined that there are occasions when a very heavy burden is placed upon the bone builders. In a bodily disorder like chronic rheumatism the cells, in their haste, often build wildly and not wisely, and in the unusual effort they dissolve into a gummy substance which cannot be taken into the blood stream and purified, and the patient feels the pain induced by the undissolved excess. When the ends of tendons and ligaments are injured or torn, the wound often is invaded by disease germs, in which case the body protects itself from the contamination by sealing that portion. The parts then become stiff and unpliable. To loosen the injured section it is well for the individual to gradually work and stretch the member, for this will revive the inflow of lubricants. Artificial heat is often applied to the parts so that the blood circulation may be encouraged, and when the blood circulates it gives material to the bone builders.

The skeleton asserts itself in giving some shape to the body. It clothes itself with the more rounded muscles and is the basic feature in holding the body erect. The bone of the skull protects the delicate fibers of the brain, and the ribs and shoulder blades protect the heart and lungs. The bones relieve the weight of the shoulders from pressing on the lungs, and the protecting ribs are flexible so as to assist in the work of the respiratory organs.

The Muscles

The muscles and ligaments hold the body together. If it were not for them the bones would fall apart. The total weight of the muscles is perhaps half of that of the body, and while they do bulk large they also perform a large work. They are great feeders, requiring a constant supply of fuel, and they consume large quantities of the products made in the body. Muscle is a semifluid substance, in which molecules group and regroup incessantly. By the movements of the body the muscles continuously extend and contract and they become fatigued. This drag is due to a waste product called lactic acid, a bitter, sirupy compound. An important material is oxygen, which is brought in quantities to the muscles by the red blood cells. There is a constant chemical change taking place in the muscles, for it is here that much heat is generated, and this heat assists the bodily mechanism. There are other heat producers, such as the liver, intestines, kidneys and the brain. The heart, for instance, transforms only one-fourth of its fuel into effective work—the balance goes into heat. The fuel used by the muscles is the glycogen which is produced by the liver. The bodily organism regulates the heat producers by some automatic process unknown to science. There are muscles wrapped around the nerve fibers and around the blood vessels. These are exceedingly pliable and tenuous. As most of the pressures in the body are due to the loosen-

ing and tightening of muscles, they are exceedingly
important in the regulating of bodily heat. The body
insists on maintaining a temperature of 98° F. and to
preserve this warmth it employs many methods. When
the temperature goes down, shivering will begin and
this stirs up the muscles so that heat generates. If the
cold persists, then the body consumes some of its excess
fat, and it closes the pores of the skin by a nerve and
muscle action, so that no heat can escape. On hot days
the skin opens its windows and doors, but on cold days
it stops up all of the openings. On hot days, in addition
to opening its doors, it also opens the sweat glands so
that evaporation of the fluids will assist in the cooling
process. All of these activities are of the muscles.

The Heart

The heart operates wholly within the body, that is,
it receives all of its material from within, and delivers
it to all parts of the body. It is the organ which may
be said to be continually on errands of mercy; its largest product is heat, but it does manufacture some fine
secretions. It is the central pumping station of the
body. The ingenuity of its construction, delicacy and
perfection of its regulation, and the effectiveness of its
operations are unequaled by any organic structure in
the created universe. The heart is placed between the
lungs, with which it continually coöperates in a symbiotic union. Every pump must have its valves, and the
intricate valves of the heart almost defy description.
The work of forcing out the pure blood and drawing
in the impure blood keeps the valves in constant motion. The blood flows in one direction only, and after
circling the body and reaching all parts it keeps on
until it finally comes back to the central station. When
the blood returns it is loaded with impurities, it has

departed from the left side of the heart as pure blood, and it returns to the right side of the heart for processing.

The valves can change size and can accommodate extra loads. They are constructed in three parts called cusps; they open or shut as conditions demand, for an active athlete will make larger calls on the heart than would a person who is at rest. In the active person the blood circulates with greater speed than when the person is quiet. In the heart there is a diastole, or expanding action, and a systole, or contracting movement. One valve permits the impure blood to flow to the large field of the lungs, where it is revitalized by taking on oxygen after the cells have discharged the impurities. The impure blood which the right auricle has received from the veins is next discharged into the right ventricle, and from there it is shot across the tissues of the lungs, and after purification it flows to the left auricle, then to the left ventricle, and from there the arteries carry it to the capillary fields of the body. At each heart beat of an active athlete the left ventricle forces seven ounces of blood into the aorta, which beautifully controls the rapid movement. There is no jerky or intermittent action. As the human body contains over one gallon of blood, it may be imagined how regular and rapid is the flow.

Going now to the extreme end of the vascular system we discover a network of fine channels, having transparent walls, and so narrow that the red blood disks must pass in single file. From these channels the tissue is irrigated and nourished by the blood cells, and the body is constantly revitalized. The arteries are the large viaducts carrying the pure blood to the capillary fields, and the veins pick up the vitiated impurities and bring them back to the right side of the heart. The capillary network, covering every portion of the body, is an important feature of the vascular system. If the human body could be stripped of everything save this network, it would reproduce or retain the perfect human shape. It is from this network that the muscles are provided with sustenance and oxygen, and from it the bone builders draw their material needs. Every organ of the body is a sponge formed of capillaries, with corpuscular cells flowing within the mesh. Beginning in exceedingly microscopic forms, the lines of network increase in size as they approach the heart. All along the system are valves worked by the muscles, and guided by the nerve messages. The large valves are composed of muscle cylinders arranged in overlapping spirals. The arteries are thicker and have less valves, and the veins are more transparent and with valve controls to prevent impure blood from receding.

There is a tremendous pressure of force at the aorta, assisted by a drawing of the blood to themselves by the spongelike organs and tissues. Every organ of the body has its individual beat and pulsation. It is said that over four pints of blood pass the aorta every minute. The body is an organic unit and every part is sustained by a mutual coöperation. There are no lazy-bones or parts, for all are in coördinated relationship. When the work becomes heavy, the adrenal glands inject adrenalin which stimulates action, and the liver under this stimulant throws a form of sugar into the blood, and the blood stream carries it to its destination. The heart functions unceasingly. It is active night and day.

In the larger view the heart is a self-sacrificing worker. It gives its all to the body. It is like love, which gives itself to the beloved. Not only does the heart ask nothing in return for its services, but it makes a further sacrifice by taking on the burden of the body's impurities. No wonder the ancients regarded the heart as the seat of love. They could not understand fully its mode of operation and attributed to the blood a special gift of animal spirits. This liquid was supposed to be a product of the brain which was infused in the blood. Louis Agassiz was accustomed to lay stress upon the obvious, pointing out that the commonplace was very apt to be the most important of all, and should by no means be omitted from our enumeration in drawing up a plan of the general scheme of things. It is acknowledged that we have the main facts of bodily function, and when we differ it is in the interpretations.

The Respiratory System

Surrounding the body on all sides is a great volume of air, which exerts a powerful pressure. Not only does the skin protect the body from too great a strain, but each cell and tissue has its outer lining. The air supplies the body with valuable life-giving elements. The old Greek philosophers spoke of pneuma as the primitive substance and the breath of life. We have carried the word-stem into our vocabulary of medical and industrial terms; a pneumatic machine is one which utilizes compressed air, and pneumonia is an infection of the lungs.

Breathing, or respiration, is centered chiefly in the lungs, which extend on either side of the heart, but there is also respiration in other parts of the body. In a biologic study of the human body we find that surfaces, internal and external, and surface energies, are of vast importance. Organs and cells which are relatively small have extensive surfaces. Chemical actions, oxidations, reductions, synthesis and hydrolytic decompositions, are all surface actions. In the lungs there are countless air chambers, and it is estimated that there are something like 725 million of the little pockets called alveoli. Under personal excitement the lungs operate rapidly, at other times when the individual is in deep thought they are very quiet and the movement is unnoticed. On an average they exhaust and fill perhaps seventeen to twenty times a minute. The fresh and cool air comes in, but the exhaust is moist and heated, and the carbon dioxide which the body cannot use is forced out. The breath does not carry out more than one-tenth of the bodily heat. Vegetable growths, especially trees and shrubbery, are very helpful to man for they free the oxygen, and human life would be impossible if there were no vegetation.

The organs and tissue of the body require large supplies of oxygen, which is carried to them by the red disks in the blood. The lungs are protected in their work by the bones and the ribs, and the muscles of the shoulders keep the weight from falling on them. Beneath, the muscular walls of the abdomen hold up and support the lungs. With no conscious effort on our part, it is surprising to note how the structures and operations of coördinating members are set in motion at each breath taken into the body.

The air comes in through the nose or mouth; on the way it is warmed and little chambers with corrugated radiators filter and moisten it. Much care is exercised so that nothing harmful enters, and there are nerve centers which examine and sample the air. On the way down the air passes two muscular doorways, which open for the air and close out the food, and then reverse the order. When an irritant slips in, the feeling is one of suffocation. The second doorway is called the glottis. It is triangular in shape and has sliding curtains on either side. The curtains swing inward and close when an irritating vapor comes to them, and we therefore gasp for breath. There is a delicate mechanism which controls the even distribution of air as it enters the corridors which lead to each lung. The lungs could not work so rapidly if they were not provided· with expansive surfaces within small spaces. The same principle prevails in other breathing organisms, such as trees, which have immense leaf surfaces, and also in the roots with their small fibers and capillaries. It is by means of these surfaces that the human body can absorb, secrete and excrete, in a moment of time. The lungs ordinarily take in a gallon of air at each breath. One-third of this is retained in the body, and the balance expelled. This large consumption of air will explain why many persons cannot be comfortably housed in a small room. It is true that few persons employ the full lung capacity. Usually only one-tenth of it is exercised, but the body has provided for unusual occasions such as undue excitement or severe efforts as in distance running.

Respiration is a very complicated process, although it appears to be very simple. The process can be called intellectual, for there is a large measure of discrimination and selection, with an equally wise provision for distribution of product. The lungs, like the alimentary system, reach outside the body for their food. It required some two hundred years for chemists and biologists to discover the actual function of the lungs. We know now that combustion and respiration are complementary processes, and that combustion and oxidation take place largely, not in the lungs, but in the muscular tissue of the body. The in-breathed air contains 21 per cent of oxygen, and this is carried to the muscles by the red disks of the blood stream. They line up against the walls of the lung chambers and absorb about 80 per cent of oxygen, and this is carried to the tissues and unloaded. The rate of breathing is determined by the percentage of oxygen and carbon dioxide contained in the blood.

The human body varies in degrees of efficiency; 25 per cent of efficiency is regarded as normal. The body is therefore capable of greater work, and the reserve force is called out on occasions of great stress and excitement. Sometimes foreign substances get into the air corridors, and even get by the two protecting gates. This is true where dust circulates, as in mines, mills and factories. These impurities accumulate on the walls of the air-passages. To remove this excess and obstruction, microscopic scavengers called phagocytes are sent out and they enjoy the cleaning-up process. The material is dissolved into mucus and is then easily removed. Thus the body has its chimney-sweeps and white-wings.

The mysteries of life lie concealed in the small units, individually of microscopic size, called cells. The cells, wherever found, are congeries of minute and discrete chemical factories, working together in harmony and related by the special work in hand. The living cells of the body are entirely different from the systems of the laboratory test tubes, and carry on manifold processes which are only partly understood.

That there is an intimate relationship between the brain and the respiration of the lungs was set forth in the Amsterdam publication, *The Economia,* as early as the year 1741, was taken up by Schlichting in 1750, by Doctor Piegu in 1846, and by others. They claimed that there is a coinciding motion of the brain with the respiration, and that the lungs, and the brain with the medulla oblongata and spinalis, have synchronous animations and spirations, the lungs rising at the precise moments that the brain inspires its costal and sympathetic nerves. The lungs are therefore excited at the same time the nerve centers are disturbed, the thought and emotion of the mind having close contacts and influence on the body.

The Glands and Hormones

Several years ago I was attracted to the study of the glands while at the St. Petersburg University, and there are many matters of interest which the layman should know. The impressive fact is that the many parts, organs and cells are admirably regulated in a coöperative harmony to the development and growth of the human body from its infancy, and that they never disagree while in health. One of Æsop's fables illustrates the truth that it will never do for the various members of the body to fall out with one another. There is a well-understood mutual dependence, a *consensus partium*. The same idea was used by one of the elder Roman statesmen when a revolt of the plebeians threatened to destroy the administration. He called the leaders together and asked them what would happen if the feet would insist on ruling the head, and if the heart would rebel at the movement of the hands. They soon saw the point and all went to work busily and in harmony.

It has been known that the brain has centers of nervous impulse from which and by which communications are established with all parts of the body. In the year 1905 there was discovered a new method of communication as established between organs and by which they coördinated their functions. In the body there are special organs of internal secretion from which little packages of chemical content, called hormones, are put into the blood stream and sent to designated stations. When some tissue or organ is in need of hormones

it sends an order and receives in due time the chemical package. The hormones are then put to work and
create unusual chemical reactions. The muscles send
messages by means of the carbon-dioxide carriers while
they are on the way to the lungs, and the white cells
of the blood are also employed in the service.

The glands of internal secretion are very small and
are located in different parts of the body; the adrenal
at the kidneys, the thyroid in the front part of the
neck, the pituitary at the base of the brain, the pancreas
close to the stomach and intestines, and in communication with the sex organs. The hormones excite and
stimulate chemical action, and they create ferments
the residue of which is eliminated. It is a general chemical rule that substances act together, and when one
substance acts upon another, it in turn is changed
chemically. But a catalyst retains the same chemical
composition and does not undergo any change; here we
have a seeming violation of the rule. The whole subject of fermentation is based upon chemical changes induced by microbes and bacteria. Carbon monoxide and
disulphide paralyze the catalysts, but as this matter is
more concerned with disease we may speak of it later.

It is well to know also that many organs and tissues
have a secreting function. The heart produces a substance which influences its contractions by acting on the
nerves, and the carbon dioxide from the muscles regulates the external movements of the lungs. Some hormones, especially those of the pituitary gland, stimulate
unusual growths of the bone and muscles, and giant
forms result. The food taken into the body for its
nourishment includes vegetable matter, and the vitamins of the vegetable act like hormones, and perform
many important uses which are just beginning to be
understood. There is also a vitamic force in sunlight

which assists the chemistry of the body. Thus we have hormones manufactured by the glands, and vitamins which come to the body from nature. Let us remember that there are billions of busy workers, each individual and independent, which combine their efforts to keep the body in good health. These workers never produce disease—they consistently fight it, for disease is a state of war.

Among the hormones, insulin has exceptional curative properties. Chemists have a wide and individual field when concerned with a study of the functions, normal and abnormal, of the organs of internal secretion. The admirable mechanisms of the animal body, acting harmoniously, coöperate in the development and growth of the body. There has been a rapid advance in this field. The French anatomist, Cuvier, in 1802, had an idea that specific control stations in the brain, spinal cord, and autonomic nervous system, coördinate all functional activity by a kind of telegraphic communication. This idea was in vogue for centuries. Lately (that is, within the past fifty years), chemistry has brought to light a new and different control.

To state it simply, the various mechanisms of our body employ a type of postal-service; little packets of chemicals are sent out by the organs of internal secretion and carried by the blood stream to appointed destinations. These packets are the hormones. These chemical messengers are elaborated in the endocrine organs, some of which are the ductless glands, devoid of secretory ducts, hence can perform their functions only by sending chemical packets to various organs of the body as they require them. Some of these organs, like pancreas and sex glands, enlarge their functions by producing ferments and additional agents that cause elimination. Bacteria find a useful place in the physical harmony. The human body is a vast, complicated machine of inter-related chemical and electric action.

It is interesting to note how this study of the glands, and the part they perform in the animal body, has occupied attention in the past years. Huxley, in 1870, wrote, "Of these glands nothing certain as to function is known, and we are as much in the dark as to the use of the large viscus called the spleen." These men did recognize a rise and fall in this organ, and also that the ductless glands possess an animatory motion, a systolic contraction, and a diastolic expansion. In Starling's *Elements of Physiology*, 1896, he says, "Under the title of the ductless glands a number of organs are grouped, the sole resemblance of which lies in the fact that we know very little about them." In cretinism, which is a form of idiocy, the thyroid gland is inactive or deficient. The condition may not be noticed at birth, but the child refuses to develop, although the abdomen enlarges. By discoveries of Horsley and Murray, various forms of the gland can be administered, either fresh or as glycerine extract, and astounding results are obtained—helpless and afflicted children are rescued. By the knowledge that life is molecular as well as somatic, and the development of that knowledge, we know that every bodily organ has a special quality of life of its own. It is there to do a special work; the secretion of a gland as a whole is shared in and produced by all its parts; its very cells have impressed on them the office of the complete organ.

The pituitary gland, suspended in the sella turcica, at the anterior part of the base of the skull, is a vascular and nervous organ. It has been called the chemical laboratory of the brain. It is in two parts, called choroid plexuses, each receiving a quantity of secretion which is elaborated and taken up in the blood stream.

This gland is often regarded as the most important organ in the preparation of the stream of blood, for it is the meeting place of the higher and the lower fluids of the body, which are here revitalized and charged for specific uses.

Some of the early anatomists suspected, 150 years before science began to investigate the subject, that the motion of the brain is synchronous with the respiration, and not with the action of the heart and blood circulation. Modern science has arrived at no conclusion, but grants the importance of chemical and pharmaceutic anticipations. Each part of the body has its own motion, but that the motion of the brain should be synchronous with the respiration, and not with the cardiac circulation, is a matter yet to be determined. The full bearings of this are not even realized today. For, altering our physiologic conduct, it would be found that we could add many years to life's course. It is almost impossible to avoid putting scientific propositions in philosophic form. Plainly, science is entitled to say, without transcending her province: first, gravitation and material substance are proportionate one to another, coördinate with one another, are correlated to one another and vary as one another in an ordinary way; second, the secretion of bile varies with the structure of the liver coördinately, proportionately, simultaneously successively; and third, so with the thoughts, emotions, and expression of the will, they vary with the structure of the brain and nervous system, in the same way. Philosophically it may be true that substance is procreated by gravitation in order to manifest its existence, that the need to secrete bile is the reason and cause why the liver exists, and that the necessity why thought, emotion, and the will may have a medium of expression, is the cause of the procreation of the brain and nervous system.

The theory is questioned and modern research furnishes no proof. It is claimed that one chief function of the brain is the manufacture of a fine lymph, or superfluid which enriches the blood in the formation and elaboration of the red corpuscles, and that it acts besides as the organ of ideation, will, and emotion. In hysteria and neurasthenia, an anemic condition is found, due to alterations in the cerebral ventricular fluid. The mental disturbances and perversions accompanying them, the psychic changes, can be accounted for in no other manner.

The Brain and Nerve System

One of the most complex and intricate systems of the body is that of the nerves and their centers, which project lines of communication to every least part. The nerve fibers are very small, finer than a hair, and white in color; each nerve fiber is a fine cylinder, wrapped by sheaths into bundles, and so sensitive that once wholly disconnected they perish. The small nerve of a tooth will often protect itself by building a wall against the intruding decay or metal filling, and careful dentists will not destroy a tooth nerve. Delicate as is the nerve, it divides at the end into two small branches, one for the ingoing message and one for the transmission. We speak of the brain as located in the head, but it can be truthfully said that the brain is everywhere present in the body. The nervous system is a physico-chemical organism with which the mind has intimate and direct contacts, and by means of this organism the mind controls and directs the action and movement of the body.

The brain is located at the top of the head, protected on all sides by the thick bones of the skull. It is in two main divisions, separated by a strong partition. In the upper cranial chamber, which is the larger of the two, are the cerebral lobes, one on the left and the other on the right side, and these are connected by countless nerve fibers. The operations cross one another, for the right lobe connects with the left side of the body, and the left lobe with the right half of the body. In the smaller and lower chamber, which is at the back of the head, are located the cerebellum, the medulla oblongata, and the brain stem which connects with the spinal cord. All of these contain nerve centers or stations.

The brain structure fills all of the skull, for only 7 per cent is occupied by fluids and wrappings. Twelve pairs of nerves begin at the brain stem. One set connects with the stomach, heart and lungs, and the others contact with the face. In the medulla oblongata, which is carefully protected, are the nerve centers which regulate the pumps of the heart, ventilation of the lungs, the alimentary canal, and the chemical laboratories. Attached to the brain stem and the prior mechanisms, the spinal cord continues the nerve centers down the back of the body.

The main nerve centers of the brain are not on the inside, but at the cortex or surface. The form of the cortex is in ridges or folds, and the corrugation thus increases the surface area of the brain. This order of arrangement is reversed in the spinal cord, for there the receiving centers are grouped at the center or root of the brain stem. The corrugations of the cortex are filled by the most delicate nerve fibers which lead inward to the larger communicating cables at the center of the brain. An example of this is seen in the rootlets of a plant, which are a matted network on the inside of a flower-pot, but which lead inward to the central stem of the plant. From the spinal cord emerge thirty-one pairs of nerves. The brain is mechanical and has no consciousness. It is the mind which sees, hears, thinks and acts, by means of the mechanism, for the mind is psychic and conscious of itself and all of its surroundings. The brain is more to the mind than the piano or musical instrument is to the musician, but there is a comparison which can aid us in its understanding.

Chemists, biologists and physiologists do not yet know the nature of the nutriment required by the nerve system. The finest and purest blood of the body goes to the brain. Its capillary fields are given fuel and oxygen by the arteries, and the veins draw into special channels the waste and excess. The brain space is so compact that it cannot receive a greater quantity of material than it discharges. The nerves are not common message carriers, they are not wires, and each has a distinct function. The system is unlike telephone or telegraph connections. Nerves contain fibers of two kinds, one for outgoing messages and the other for communications to the central station. The nerves no doubt transmit their messages by pulsations or tremulations, and in wave lengths. Due to the slow vital combustion, the rate of speed is only four miles per hour, but in the short distances this is relatively very rapid.

We might suppose that the bulk of the messages would concern sensations of touch, pressure, pain, heat and cold, but the fact is that the great majority are muscle messages keeping the central office informed on the conditions prevailing within the body. There are two hundred pairs of muscular engines in the body, and information is communicated from one to the other through the nerve centers. Rapid communication is essential in large and complex organizations, and civilization advances in the degree that telegraph, postal, wireless, radio, and highway construction improve. It is the intensely sensitive communicative system of the human body which makes it the outstanding organism of perfection. Imagine for the moment the operation when a particle of dust gets into the eye, an urgent message goes to the central station, from there a message comes to open the gland duct of the eye, the discharged fluid flushes the spot and the grain of dust is washed out, and a message is flashed back that conditions are again normal. The nerves become fatigued due to the constant combustion and the accumulated waste, and they recuperate when we lie down and relax or go to sleep.

Key and Retzius, taking up earlier discoveries, insist that there is a cerebrospinal liquid which circulates between the fibers of the nerves. They also contend that the choroid plexuses in the lateral ventricles consist of two leaves, of which the upper leaf is derived from the fimbria of the fornix and the lower leaf partly so. I have found no British or American authorities who agree with this formula, although it meets with approval in Russia. In a dead brain there is no indication of these facts. The channels of excretion lead down to the spinal cord from the brain. That there are two substances in the nerves is now admitted. One is white and the other gray. The office of the pituitary gland has but recently been explored, and its secretions may develop new discoveries. There is a trilogy of the cerebrum, the cerebellum, and the spinal axis. Dr. J. Luys, in his *Iconographie Photographique des centres Nerveux*, gives detailed information on the connection between the white fibers of the nerves and the gray substance of the brain.

The atmospheric pressures exerted against the surface of the body have been mentioned, and there are many forces which flow through the body which the nerves do not register. Ether waves, wireless and radio do not disturb the nerve system. The X-rays and cosmic rays can penetrate the body, but the eye does not see them nor do the nerves feel them. The invisible forces which register in the body are the emotions and the thoughts. Both of these create chemical reactions which the nerves register. As the mind of man is constructed of two substances, will and understanding, it is in them that we must search for the controlling power, for the human body is merely a mechanism by which thought and will are expressed.

Life and Death

We cannot fully understand life unless we have some knowledge of death, for as Bichat has said, "life is the sum total of forces which resist death." Science attempts to make definitions of physical laws and modes of action and control, but it is difficult to reduce the phenomena of life to fundamental equations. Just so long as the living cell, which is a discrete chemical factory, can resist the forces of decay, the human body will continue to live. Death is not caused by the enzymes of digestion, but by the materials introduced into the individual cells. Suffering and dissolution take place when the organism lags for want of oxygen. When oxidations are seriously interrupted, life cannot be restored even by artificial means of respiration. All of the organs share in the power of self-digestion. The nerve centers of the medulla oblongata, when injured or interrupted, begin to dissolve, and death ensues because the respiration and heart muscles cease to act. Death, in the human body, is strictly a chemical action. An excess of acid, or an abnormal toxic condition, produces extreme temperatures which cause the nerve cells to dissolve, and they can never be restored to function. Senility and death in old age are due to disintegration of nerve centers. Waste products accumulate, causing intense action by the phagocytes, under which the blood cells become disordered and the body cannot throw off the disease-breeding germs and bacteria.

The Skin or Limbus

The function of the skin and the films of cells, tissue, and organs are worthy of serious study. Until we arrive at an understanding of them, many of the hitherto unconquerable maladies must remain unsolved. These films or limbi play a large part in the processes of secretion and excretion. The cell doctrine, as formulated by Dutrochet, Schwann and Scheiden, before the middle of the last century, is one of the greatest scientific discoveries. Surfaces, internal and external, and surface energies are of paramount importance, and are in astonishingly large areas. These surfaces or boundaries are the seats of all manner of chemical changes. The molecular arrangement of the surfaces and their constant interaction with sources of free energy may account for the continued changes which characterize living things. The difference between life and death is one of degree, and the secret is in the action of surfaces. J. Willard Gibbs, by his fundamental and profound researches, first placed the theory of surface phenomena on a truly scientific basis. Physiologists and pharmacologists are aware of the nature of the problems concerned in the interfaces and limiting membranes of living structures.

Having made a summary of the wonderful chemicophysical operations of the human body, we may conclude that billions of individual cells are functioning in marvelous coöperative ways to develop and sustain the human organism. This organism is a machine used by some higher power, which though invisible has been expressing itself by means of the mechanism. If the human body is so complete and perfect, the higher and prior organism demands of us some explanation, for the internal and invisible can be known only from the external and the visible.

> Sudden arose
> Ianthe's soul; it stood
> All beautiful in naked purity,
> The perfect semblance of its bodily frame.

> Instinct with inexpressible beauty and grace
> Each stain of earthliness
> Had passed away, it reassumed
> Its native dignity, and stood
> Immortal amid ruin.

CHAPTER VII

MAN'S DESIRE FOR SOCIAL ORDER

We men of earth have here the stuff
Of Paradise.—We have enough;
We need no other stones to build
The stairs into the Unfulfilled,
  No other ivory for the doors,
  No other marble for the floors;
No other cedar for the beam
And dome—of man's immortal dream.

Here on the paths of every day,
Here on the common human way,
  Is all the stuff the gods would take
  To build a heaven; to mould and make
New Edens; ours the stuff sublime
To build eternity in time.

FROM earliest times when men began to live in communities, there was born the craving for an ideal government of right, justice and peace. In the minds of
the Greek philosophers the idea prevailed that government had "relationship with the best in the individual
man." Perhaps this idea came to them from the wise
men of the Euphrates valley where walled cities gathered larger populations. Could a city be built in the
form of a man, be placed part to part even as obedient
members of the human body? The structure of a man
was the model of a city. In Plato's *Commonwealth* it
is said, "Supposing the most perfect form of civil government to be an image and representation of that
internal constitution and government formed and established by nature in the mind of a good man." They

evidently regarded nature as a reliable guide, for man was a product of her handiwork and her law. These ancient statesmen were looking for a pattern, for an ideal, as a guide to perfect government. In *The Republic* we meet the same idea: "the State as the larger individual has the same virtues to be cultivated as in the individual." The thought is carried farther, for it compares possible forms of government interests with the ruling affections of the individual, and concludes that from these interests and affections the several strata of society can be defined.

The Greek philosophy had its influence on the thought of the early Christian Church. Saint Paul visions the Christ as the head of the body of the Church. "For as we have many members in one body, and all members have not the same office; so we, being many, are one body in Christ, and every one members of one another." The idea of a unified purpose, functioning under the direction of intelligent leadership, and manifesting itself in many directions, continued to sway the minds of these men. Clement of Alexandria, in A.D. 200, writes, "The Church has organic life; it is a community of men who are led by the Divine Logos, an invincible city on earth which no force can subdue. The Church is like a human being, consisting of many members; it is refreshed and grows; it is welded and compacted together; it is fed and sustained by a supernatural life, and becomes in its turn, in the hands of the divine Instructor, a means of leading humanity into life. The bond of the Church's unity, the secret of the Church's growth and life, is the living, personal Christ, whose immanence in humanity is the only force adequate to its deliverance from sin, and its final perfecting according to the original purpose of its creation." Back of these words is the implied thought that the perfect government is impossible because of the wickedness of man, and that while nature has a perfect order from the creator, the government of men can be restored only by exercise of the Divine power. The Revelation of Saint John ends in a vision of a holy city, of which the Lord is the light, its citizens are those who have overcome the evil, and in it is a tree, the leaves of which are for the healing of the nations.

We cannot free ourselves of the idea-forms developed in the wisdom of the past; they must be reconsidered in the light of new data and new possibilities; the stones of truth which they were unable to cut and polish, by modern methods may be forced to emit their precious light.

> Once in a lifetime is uttered a word
> That doth not vanish as soon as 'tis heard;
> Once in an age is humanity stirred,
> Once in a century springs forth a deed
> From the dark bands of forgetfulness freed,
> Destined to shine, and to help, and to lead.

It seems impossible that men would entertain the idea of a perfect social order, unless such an organization really existed somewhere as a pattern toward which their aspirations were directed. Were hope ever fully realized it would be the ultimation, and therefore the perfect social system may be in the world beyond, and the influx of its spirit into the world of men may be the urge that drives us on to achieve something of its pattern here on earth. Roger Bacon, five centuries ago, suggested that "There are two ways of knowing; namely, by statement and by experiment. A statement lays down, and makes us define the scope of a problem; but it neither confirms doubt nor removes it in such a way as to give one trust in the attainment of certitude, unless it arrive at the truth by way of experiment." We are compelled to gather the data by careful survey, confirm them by what we know of human society, and discover whether the light helps us in solving the sociologic problems in which we are concerned.

We may assume that man has been socially minded for the past ten thousand years, but we have no records that date back to half of that time. Preceding our known literary period there were three books, all of them lost except for a few quotations, *The Book of Jasher, The Enunciators,* and *The Wars of God.* These three volumes are mentioned in the Books of Moses. When we examine the Scriptures we are forced to conclude that the first ten chapters of Genesis are allegorical, and no doubt convey in symbolic language the summary of preceding ages. Under the personification of Adam the agricultural consciousness of the race is depicted. It was a child's era of peace, a sensitiveness to things of heaven, and a curiosity to understand the meaning of life. The eating of an unknown fruit was the development of the intellect in its search for the secret of Life. In the quest, the inconclusions arrived at by the reason are the same doubts which assail the modern man when he attempts to find God by mathematical calculations. The death of Abel at the hands of Cain is a symbol illustrative of the separation which occurs when the practical mind ignores its mystical side. When intelligence divorces love and its uses, the mind is darkened and bears its mark. The Flood of Noah is a word picture of the muddy waters of reasoning without purpose, which always ends in catastrophe. The ancient legend filled the ark with animals, but not with plants or vegetable seeds, because animals have warm blood and these correspond to the affections, meaning that the desires and affections of man survive his intellectual misconceptions. Thought may be paralyzed, but man still has love as a receptacle of Life. The rainbow of hope and courage was spanned across the dark clouds, and man began to reconstruct his adjustments to God and the universe by means of his loves. Thus are condensed in these ancient symbols and parables the eras and cultures which preceded the literary age of which we have records.

The Genesis story of human history begins with Abram because he had faith in the Divine which became the basis of the Israelitish State. The patriarchs developed this faith until Joseph went down to Egypt, and into Egypt's prison he was sold. The material success of Joseph acted as a deadening influence on the spiritual idealism of the Hebrews, and they were under a servile bondage for three hundred years. No doubt the pressure of materialistic thought was inherited from Jacob, who was always bargaining with Jehovah for personal advancement. Had Esau not sold his birthright for a mess of pottage, both Hebrew and Christian history would be different from its present form. Esau was emotional, Jacob was practical, and it is the practical which misleads the emotional. Intelligence cannot succeed without the aid of the mystical.

A comparative study of ancient legends gives us collateral evidence of their similarity, which indicates a common basis of knowledge. In the Assyrian tablets found at Nineveh, the primordial Apsu created the heavens and the earth. The abyss-female Tiamat and her brood of monsters assaulted the gods of heaven. Marduk, the son of the supreme God, slew Tiamat, and out of his own blood and bone he created man.

The fragment reads:

> In order to save them He created mankind,
> The merciful One, with whom is the calling into life.
> May He establish, and may never His word be forgotten
> In the mouth of the race whom His hands created.

In the Chaldean legend the woman Omorka presided over the darkness and the abyss of waters. The god Belus cut the woman asunder. With one-half he formed the earth, and of the other half the heavens. Belus then took off his own head, the blood gushed forth and mixed with the soil, and from thence was formed man. The Egyptian, Aryan, Greek, Latin and Scandinavian sagas have variations of this same thought. All known legends have corroborations of a golden age similar to the Biblical Eden, also of the flood, and the fall of man from his primitive innocence.

The Mosaic summary is a refined and spiritualized conception of the process of creation and the early or primitive period of human history. The cosmos is created in six periods, coming to a rest in the seventh, conveying the idea of a perfection attained through struggle; a graphic anticipation of the evolution of human character, and by means of it the ideal government. Evidently man was given this hope in the first incarnation, his spirit is destined to struggle through many vicissitudes to a final triumph, the goal of his eternal hope and effort.

The persistence of the Hebrew ideal is due to the fact that it was centered in a divinely conceived and humanly defined principle. It is the consciousness of an ideal government for men. In the patriarchal age it was centered in the tribe, where every member worked for and defended the community interests, and obeyed the guidance of the chief. When Moses revived the ideal, the division was into twelve tribes, and these had as a guiding center the Tabernacle with its veil of cloud by day and the light of fire by night. This same principle of government continued down to the time of the prophet Samuel, and the decadence of tabernacle worship under the priest Elihu. It was given another form when Saul was anointed as king and came to its next zenith under the rule of King Solomon.

Every cycle or era conceives God in the terms of its own thought. In the age of savagery, when a man wanted food or habitation, he killed animal or man that would supply his needs. It was the age of brutal force and his God became the ideal of his actions. This period was followed by that of barbarism, when men began to shape things for their own use, and human industry had faint beginnings. To the Greeks, barbarism meant a meaningless babble of sound; but it was a step in the direction of primitive education. To them, God was conceived as the creator, for this was the ideal toward which they worked. Then came feudalism, when the idea of servility entered human thought; it was the age of slavery and bondsmen. The weaker owed his existence to the lord of the manor, and out of this stage of progress was born the idea of God as the owner of all things, and man as his servant. It is interesting to note that political feudalism and baronial power were overwhelmed in the Wars of the Roses. Then came the state of monarchy, in which the idea of God as king prevailed. All of these seemingly diverse ideas are retained in the records of the Bible, for in it are woven the threads of all human experience. Monarchy placed God as the ruler on a throne, but democracy working more closely to the ideals of Jesus brought God down as a living Presence among men. Perhaps we are now approaching the stage of the benevolent dictator, combined with the idea that property and goods belong to all of the people regardless of class distinction. But, out of the new era will come a new concept of God, a nearer approach to reality. The idea of a perfect government runs like a silver thread all through the idealism of the Christian teaching. Jesus Christ held up the ideal of the Kingdom of Heaven, and the most widely repeated prayer among men contains the plea, Thy kingdom come. This kingdom is spiritual and not material; if it were of this world then would my friends fight for it, and even angels, according to the word of Jesus given to Pilate. Granted that there is a spiritual government, divinely ordered and coördinated, in what measure can human intelligence understand its principles and embody them in a social order made after the discovered pattern? To what extent and with what success can a spiritual reality work itself out in human affairs and thus demonstrate its superiority and power?

One of the epoch-making books of the world is *The Republic of Plato*; the first English edition was published by Foulis at Glasgow in 1763. It attracted no notice until reprinted in 1804. Jowett, in reviewing the book, says, "Nothing actually existing in the world, at all resembles Plato's ideal State, nor does he himself imagine such a State is possible." Plato had passed through trying experiences which were well calculated to make him mistrust all existing forms of political systems. He may have projected the idea of the *Republic* as a protest, or he may have labored under the age-old longing for a just social order. In the year 1600, Lord Bacon published his book, *The New Atlantis,* a philosophic allegory in which an ideal form of government is discovered on a mythical island, to the shores of which the wind has blown the ship of voyagers. It recounts their experiences as they are introduced to the customs of the natives, and their astonishment at the orderly government under which these people live and thrive.

In the past as in the present, students of government and thinkers who have been appalled by the waste of human effort have tried to evolve some practical line of action which would free us of the burdens of misrule. Sensitive and far-seeing men have always rebelled at the manifest misgovernment of the people, and have attempted to discourage and defeat the evils and ills of their day, and to discover some form of leadership which would establish economical and equitable political conditions. The difficulties to be faced are not due to the low state of intelligence of the masses, an ignorance which can be overcome by education, but to the universal desire inherent in every individual to serve his personal interests at all costs. The predominant thought in every mind is that, if we are to succeed in attaining our own comfort and convenience, we must fight for them, and in this struggle every man is our foe. No modern form of government makes the welfare and comfort of all of its citizens the first consideration. The people must support the government, but the government cannot be expected to support the people. Governments are formed to defend us from foreign enemies, and to protect our property. The individual and community welfare, its physical, ethical and spiritual happiness, is not a consideration of the government. Hospitals, welfare associations, higher institutions of learning, churches, the press, and the stage, all of the forces which go toward building character in the individual, are supported and managed by groups of individuals, and what they have created is taxed by the State. The national governments have

wasted the earnings of the people in wars, they have
sacrificed human lives to perpetuate their own forms,
they have encouraged the idea that every man must
fight for his own self-preservation. The fundamental
principle on which government is now organized is
wrong in conception and destructive in operation.

There is no national appeal to the unused talent of
its people, no encouragement to that feeling deep in
the soul of man, that he wants to do right in all of his
relations with other men, and that his only safety and
success are realized when all men are happy and satisfied.

> What asks our Father of His children save
> Justice and mercy and humility,
> A reasonable service of good deeds,
> Pure living, tenderness to human needs,
> Reverence, and trust, and prayer for light to see
> The Master's footsteps in our daily ways?
> No knotted scourge, nor sacrificial knife,
> But the calm beauty of an ordered life,
> Whose every breathing is unworded praise.

The defeat of righteous conduct is inevitable under
modern political conditions, the burden of dishonesty
and crime is largely on the State, for it puts every
member at warfare with his brother; divides class
against class, the poor against the rich, and the innocent are left to suffer the iniquity of the criminal. This
may appear like a severe indictment, because it indicts
a nation, but the facts justify the conclusion. Governments do not command the best in man. If they did
we would have peace and not war. They do not encourage the welfare of every member of the community. If they did we would have prosperity and not
adversity. Nature has provided lavishly for the suste-

nance of man, but the human organization has defeated nature's provision.

What we need to recover is a spiritual idea as a pattern for the solution of the problems confronting social government. The evolution of the family into the tribe, the tribe into a federation, the federation into the nation, and the international relationships has been a gradual process, and this slow order of development brings us to the next era of government. A statesman remarked, "Yesterday, and ever since history began, men were related to one another as individuals. Today the common relationships are largely with great impersonal concerns, with organizations, not with other individuals. Ours is a new social age, a new era of relationships, a new setting for the drama of life." The advance of civilization has come because intelligent men solve the problems facing the race, and thus the enigma of life yields its secrets. Each succeeding culture gains its victories and thus the art of thinking and living is enhanced.

In the thirteenth century architecture and painting, by an inquisitive artistic adjustment, came into new triumphs; in the fifteenth century the printing press multiplied books which distributed knowledge to more minds; in the sixteenth century religion and the Church were compelled to find new adjustments, classic manuscripts were made available to scholars in Europe and England; in the seventeenth century the new science was awakened and men began to discern between what is sure, what is likely and what is possible. The accurate study of natural phenomena displaced credulity and superstition. Science began as a faith, it developed into reason, and then became certitude. To-day we find this planet small and limited; there are new categories of human faith and of mental possibilities. The accumulated knowledge gives us faith in an ultimate solution of the problem of man, his purpose in the plan of existence, and a discovery of his final destination.

Man has come into his own self-consciousness, and communities must do the same. The government we create is the legal expression of human thought, and we cannot expect any form of government to be in advance of its own best minds. When rulers are chosen or elected, or ordained by hereditary right, they do not become thereby transformed in character; they carry with them into office the same ideas and habits which they acquired in previous years. There is no instance of an ignorant man who, having good intentions and given the power to enforce them, has not finally done more harm than good. The executive type of mind is composed of native ability, trained and educated. The official is the servant, either of the better element which elected him, or of the special interests or unsocial factions, that take advantage of his cupidities.

Every thing in the world is old, the only new things that come into it descend through the minds of men. Whenever there has been a development of the arts and sciences in the past centuries, its inception was born in the minds of those men who devoted their lives to serious thinking. The culture, modes and customs, attitudes toward things, and the use of natural resources continually change because of human discoveries and inventions. After the new ideas and new processes are proven and find acceptance, the old credulities, antiquated methods, and earlier superstitions are discarded and forgotten. Such is the mind of man; it adapts itself first to its own thought and then to the new environment. When we examine a plant, an animal, or a mineral, our thought should be, What did the Creator plan as its ultimate use when He formed it? If we could lift its covering, understand the nature of its structure and operation, we could hear a voice speaking to our skill and ingenuity, begging us to coöperate with Him in utilizing it for the greater service of mankind. Nature in its manifold forms is full of little windows through which we should see the future glory and power that it is suggesting to us.

> They do not tell some truth untold
>   To this new day;
> They tell some truth already old
>   In some new way.
> The truth forever must be shown,
>   If new or not;
> For there is nothing much unknown,
>   But much forgot.

Serious study of vegetation was not begun until 1680, when the chemical action and formation of plants were first observed. The circulation of the blood attracted no scientific interest until the year 1599. Nature was supposed to consist of but five elements of matter previous to 1850. The telephone, auto, airplane, radio, X-ray, helium and radium are in common use to-day, but sixty years ago they were unknown and the world went on its way without them. What brought them into the world? The needs of modern man? This is scarcely true, for need can never create, but it may stir the mind to find a satisfaction. The mind of man delved into its inner chambers for ideas, it reached into the Unknown, and the unknown replied. In the quest for an answer someone notes the mysterious working of nature's law and studies its behavior, or finds some unknown element and begins to experiment. These studies and experiments are followed and tested by other men, and the secret is gradually disclosed. Progress and civilization are the result of logical and determined thinking. The human mind has access to a reservoir of substantial entities not of this world, from whence it draws what it needs at the moment. Scientists have generally held to the doctrine of independent evolution; which means that the same thing occurs in different parts of the world. When a man in Asia has an idea of something new, the chances are that men in other parts of the world will arrive at the same discovery, independent of each other.

Mayan architecture is in many ways like that of Egypt and Persia, but there is no evidence that one side of the world knew what the other was building. Fish and birds in the Pacific will have habits similar to those in the Atlantic. Every wasp builds her clay house of ten chambers, and she has never had a teacher. If ideas occurred only once, and were never repeated, there would be many gaps which could never be bridged. The probable truth is that ideas are pressing through to us from the higher and interior world, and minds attuned to their vibrations register the inspirations. No great invention belongs solely to one man, for he never works alone; the combined genius of men produces or reproduces that which comes by intimation from inner sources. The one thing that seems certain is that the human race must find its own way, must build its own house, must hew out of the unknown the substances from which to carve its temples and habitations. We have some of the plans and blue-prints discoverable in different parts of our mental dimensions which can be gathered and studied for guidance. The pattern of the celestial systems, each in its solitary flight, yet bound together by threads of invisible cosmic rays and magnetic, electric atoms; the orderly structures of the bees, wasps and ants, found in their terraced workshops and dwellings; the operations of the human mind, and the marvelous functions of the human body; each and all may yield to science the mystery of coherent and adjusted organization of social government.

The Kingdom of Heaven, as faintly outlined in the Scriptures, suggests the spiritual dimensions; and the slow evolution of human government given to us in the history of race culture forms a basis for more secure buildings on their foundations. Let us pursue our studies in silence, for

There may be moving among us, curious people and races,
Folk of the fourth dimension, folk of the vast star spaces.
   They may be trying to reach us,
   They may be longing to teach us
   Things we are longing to know.
     If it is so,
   Voices like these are not heard in earth's riot;
     Let us be quiet.

Classes with classes disputing, nation warring with nation,
Building and owning, and seeking to lead—this is not all!
   Endless the works of creation,
   There may be waiting our call
   Beings in numberless legions,
   Dwellers in rarefied regions,
   Journeying Godward like us,
   Alist for a word to be spoken,
   Awatch for a sign or a token,
     If it be thus,
   How they must grieve at our riotous noise
   And the things we call duties and joys!

Let us be silent for a little while;
Let us be still and listen. We may hear
Echoes from other worlds not far away.

CHAPTER VIII

TUNING IN ON THE OTHER WORLD

When we tune in on the Spiritual World what do we discover? There is nothing strange or unusual in its activities and affairs, for our experiences in this world have been in training for its advent, and unconsciously we have been prepared for our individual place in its dominion. The manner in which it expresses life is in accord with the universal principle which we have observed in our physical bodies, and in the operations of our organized mind. The three organisms, body, mind, and spirit, function on parallel lines; their order and sequence is of vital concern to man for they constitute his response to Life.

Each organism contains systems which perform specific tasks, and in their combined and mutual operations they sustain their community interests and welfare. The three organisms grow and develop by a selective process of absorbing food and fuel, and adapting these nutriments for the welfare of their existence. They all reject elements and substances which are foreign to their uses and needs, and thus exhibit a remarkable discrimination and judgment. The ability of choice and adaptation indicates a consciousness of their own needs, a sense of values and purpose, and the perception of an ultimate goal. When we inquire why all growing things pursue the extraordinary behavior of this type, there is no adequate answer unless we admit that there is a well-defined plan in life as a whole.

When salt or sugar crystals begin to form, the particles assume a geometric precision which is remarkably accurate and uniform; when the saturate solution evaporates, the minute parts obey an established rule of order from which they never depart. Among plants there is the same obedience to law and order; in the single flower the marginal petals subordinate their efforts for the welfare of the group, for each one, if uncontrolled, would develop into a complete flower. They do not mature and ripen seeds, but sacrifice their cycle of existence so that pollen-carrying insects may be attracted to the fringe of the beautiful flower of which they have become minor parts. There is every reason for believing that there is a sociologic basis in the scheme of things which combines efforts in fighting predacious and parasitic enemies. Plant forms often enter into partnerships, as in the lichen, where the microscopic alga joins with the fungus for mutual welfare. The alga is involved in the mycelium of the fungus and manufactures for its partner organic food, while the fungus as its share supplies the alga with essential salt solutions. By this marriage the combined plant can exist in many situations which would be death if they were separated. The lichen, the result of the combination, is one of the hardiest plant structures in nature.

When we examine the processes of the human body we find the same coöperative service; should any member be injured, the blood cells rush in and fill the gap, thus reconstructing the original form. The cells sacrifice themselves in the task. Some remain fixed as muscle or skin, while others carry away the broken and poisonous matter and perish under the weight of the load. This universal obedience to service indicates provision, plan, and purpose in the expression of life. The history of any people will furnish multitudes of examples where men and women have given undivided attention and energy for the good of society, seeking no visible reward, and regarding their efforts as the least they could do for their fellows. This insistent urge, inherent everywhere in life, to maintain organized society, cannot be dismissed from serious consideration when we study man and his unusual behavior under invisible forces of necessity.

Involved in all forms of growth are the problems of food, and when we examine the particular food which it selects we are helped in our understanding of the structural elements of the organism. The human body secures its food and fuel from the elements and atmospheres of the material world, which furnish the only supply. The human mind obtains its food from the sensory activities of the body; through the eye and ear it gathers information; in observing its own reactions it acquires method and technique; within its own reason it forms conclusions, and from beyond its consciousness it registers stimuli that form motives. The food of the Kingdom of Heaven comes to it in the form of aspirations, abilities and talents, which have been developed by individuals through experience and practice in this world. By a rare selective process the Kingdom of Heaven combines these individual talents for a coöperative service, and evolves higher forms of goodness and truth, and thus grows into a perfection which could not be achieved by the lower organisms. Thus the three organisms are complementary, and this explains the constant effort of man to fit into his appointed order, and to attain his most eminent goal. None can ignore the fact that there has been battle and conflict all along the ascent, for enemies have been active from the beginning, and their strategy and type have altered with the circumstances. In all births the problem of death is to be faced, but man by his inherent nature insists on the enjoyment of life regardless of the ferocity of destructive agencies. In all three organisms the food is converted into new forms which · in no manner resemble their original structure and arrangement, and the simpler forms always sacrifice themselves to meet the higher requirements. The constant urge in crystals, solids and liquids, and in all elements, is in the direction of superior uses, and the principle of action is universal.

The human body builds on a foundation of bone and cartilage, and over this framework it lays a series of muscles which are pliable and sinuous, and by their means the bones are coördinated and controlled. The bodily structure is protected by layers of skin, which hold the organism together, and cushion it from the pressure of the atmosphere. Within the framework, and as part of it, are the heart and lungs, co-partners engaged in purifying and renewing the entire system. The wonderful mechanism of the body centers control and direction in the brain, heavily protected by the skull, and the small fibers in the cortex of the brain communicate with the mind, and thus the physical and the mental come to a common focus. The goal which the body has in view is the perfection of its own organism, and the subordination of all of its parts and functions is to this one end.

The human mind has three compartments or planes: it absorbs at the lower level the facts and general information carried to it by the bodily senses. The sense impressions, scientific facts, and pragmatic knowledges furnish thought to the second plane of the mind, where new connotations are developed, and ideas are classified and grouped. The third plane of the mind is engaged in philosophic and spiritual contemplation and refines all the material which comes to it from beneath, and struggles to harmonize it with the invisible self. By this ascent from the material world and its sensations to the sublime heights of spirit, the fully developed individual attempts to tune his experiences to the rhythm of the Kingdom of Heaven.

Following the same procedure, the Kingdom of Heaven draws to itself all of the refined values which have been developed and accumulated in the fields below it. It uses the simple and less responsive elements which come to it as a basis for its own structure, and by methods of segregation and adaptation creates pure and harmonious substances which function within the protected precincts. The process of refinement and sublimation is a constant effort to perpetuate its organism and perfect its operations. The coördinated activities of the Kingdom of Heaven continually create new forms for expressing the higher incentives of life, and the benefits which accrue are shared not only by the organism of heaven but by all forms beneath its province.

All life is a unit, and its final expression is in man; the more perfect man becomes the more diversified and complete is the expression. It is well for man to recognize that within himself there are unused powers of unusual ability, and these inner potential forces once aroused will seek expression in various forms outside himself. Effects reveal causes to a close observer, and man must discover his inner self in the order and system which he is attempting to establish in the world under his control. In the course of historic events we can see how the human will has tried to express itself in behavior, and by a study of the order which prevails in the universe we can imagine something of the order which is possible within ourselves, for man is related to his universe. The doctrine of evolution has helped us in understanding that order, for there are unlimited varieties of creatures, and there is an unbroken relationship between the simplest forms at the bottom to the complex form of man. The fact that forms have changed, and that many forms have disappeared, proves that when they are incapable of adjusting themselves to world conditions, they lose the power of reproduction and become extinct.

When we regard life in the terms of use and service, it is possible to understand that each creature is the embodiment of its use in the adaptation of its own functions to the life of the whole. Each has the power to convert into forms those elements which express its use, and the limit of its existence depends on the measure of its service. The species and varieties which render service have a prolonged existence, but where functions have been perverted they have suffered degradation, and this has limited their activities.

Stopford Brooke, contemplating our failures, says, "It is our feebleness, our ignorance, our want of life, our inability to give fine form to thought and feeling, that make our disquiet. The more of life, the more rest; the swifter the creation, the more peace; the quicker the spinning of the sphere, the quieter the sphere." Phillips Brooks is impressed by the beauty of service as satisfaction, when he says: "The shortness of life is bound up with its fullness. It is to him who is most active, always thinking, feeling, working, caring for people and for things, that life seems short. Strip a life empty and it will seem long enough." Edward Carpenter suggests the harmony attained by orderly effort, "To create around oneself an external world which answers to the world within, is indeed a great happiness, and the fulness of Life. To express oneself, to bring all the elements of one's nature into harmony and then to . . . build them out into the actual world, into a means of union with others: how glorious that were."

Man can come into an understanding of those things which belong to the world below himself because he is more complete and more highly gifted than they are, and he can see the relationship of that which is beneath to that which is above himself. He can therefore adapt himself to conditions, and create in them new situations impossible of attainment by any other creature. He can extend his thoughts and affections far beyond the limits of his body, he is subject to moods which have no perceptible or physical basis, he can entertain aspirations and exercise perceptions which probe the depths of the unconscious and produce an awareness of unlimited resources. Sustenance of the physical is important, but more essential are the intangibles which are continually produced and shared by man. Such are the substances of esthetic and spiritual value, the accretions of a charitable mind, the states produced by tender sympathies, unselfish loves, and unawarded kindnesses that are silently expressed in daily actions. He has within his uses not only the gift of survival, but he has the ability to accumulate the wisdom and the experiences of the ages, and to mold them into fixed forms of literature, of music, of institutions, and mechanisms, so that they become the heritage of his posterity. He has the marvelous faculty of capitalizing his personal and group experiences. Theodora Thompson says, "There are vast stores of untapped energy and extraordinary possibilities lying latent within each one of us, only waiting the necessary consciousness to call them forth—endless precious faculties which, if developed and brought to light, would mean a veritable

rebirth for the individual. And not until man learns to
enrich his mundane existence by the fuller possession
of himself and his surroundings, and a greater intensity of conscious life, by the development of a deeper
and stronger individuality, and by using his God-given
powers of vision and perception, will he experience this
rebirth."

Man is unconsciously striving to express the finer
values within himself in the social systems external to
himself, and this urge is the motive of all of his efforts
to perfect the governmental and political order, regardless of the repeated failures he has endured. As
these systems now exist they have failed to satisfy his
longings, because there is no agreed plan or concerted
and intelligent movement, and this brings him to an
impasse so long as he is ignorant of the unified organization possible in his own inner life. The spirit of man
must be regimented and controlled before social order
can be systematically organized.

If people have traits worthy of valuation as elements in national solidarity, they demand recognition;
they plead with the masses everywhere, and they call
for opportunity for everyone. Humanity is not a mass
of dross with an occasional vein of gold running
through it, for the common continent of mankind is
impregnated with most precious treasures. Give it favorable conditions and it will treat itself; it will clarify
and polish itself by means of its own spirit expressed
in the genius of human relations.

The mental and spiritual evolution of man is just as
certain as is his physical evolution. The wisdom of the
sages marks the mileposts along the path he has trav-
eled. In the early ages of this evolution man was over-
awed by the changing phenomena of nature and cowed
in fear before them. In that period his religious con-

cepts were the product of that fear; he fashioned idols which personified his nature deities, and offered gifts to appease their wrath. To a child, nature is a teacher with an open book, but to one who violates her laws she is an avenging monster. Therefore, the innocent age of the first race was followed by the decadent age of human sacrifice and idol worship. Man has fortunately survived many changes; his world has changed to conform to his mental persuasions. In these modern days he has come into a fuller knowledge of himself and of the universe, but he has momentarily been intrigued into believing that the power of control is not within himself. False prophets would convince him that life has no meaning, and that he is the victim of a blind Fate, and that adventurous struggle is futile. He has yet to learn that there are superior powers above and within his own attainment, and until he discovers this higher order and avails himself of his coöperation, he will fail in perfecting the social system of his government. The only release from mental and social tyranny is in the unification of the forces of service.

Obstacles are to be regarded as incentives to action. What is taking place on this earth is a great experiment in the development of human character. The problem is not one of money, markets, or physical comforts, but the production of real and enduring men. We have enough of undeveloped races that easily exist where food is bountiful and clothing unnecessary. It is always the trials, problems, and a measure of suffering which develop the best in men; and there are antagonistic forces active both in the individual and in society. The principle of organic unity is fundamental in sociology; society is a coöperative association of individuals, molded by the compulsion of economic neces-

sity, but primarily actuated by the higher principles of
brotherly love. The effectiveness of society depends on
orderly organization, and the State possesses the same
attributes that come to a trained individual who practices the higher values.

Every individual and every society is confronted by
three main problems which affect its existence; food,
which is essential to growth and health; protection,
which involves the conservation of its energies; purpose, which means the direction of energy to the
achievement of a definite end. Every social system is
composed of parts, and while it may seem that the
individual's liberties are limited, yet the organization
grants him a freedom and independence, and a means
of development of personal talent, impossible outside
its realm.

An individual may set himself in opposition to the
social system, and the more developed a system is, the
more does the opposition appear to assert itself; for
its perfection demands qualities and talents which the
individual may not possess. Contrary to Ibsen's dicta,
that the strongest man is he who stands most entirely
alone, the facts are that the personal freedom within
the social system provides opportunities and compensa-
tions not obtainable by isolation. Temporary inactivity
is one of the rules of order, there are functions of the
highest order which are not called into action by the
body except at unusual moments; there are intellectual
areas of the mind which remain cloistered until opportunity opens; there are segregated groups in the professions that require a long training for service; and
there are remnants of buried values in the childhood
of the human race that will be recovered to meet the
needs of some future crisis; there are lost ages, cultures, and peoples, but some day the explorer will find

and tabulate their secreted arts. Phillips Brooks said,
"Life comes before literature, as the material always
comes before the work. The hills are full of marble
before the world blooms with palaces."

Every nationality has its own acquired and inherent
types and characteristics, and the social life of the
world is constantly changed by vital accretions. Governments follow the form of their constitutions, but it is
always the citizen who makes the constitution. Language, social customs, and national character develop
by absorption of individual characteristics into the
larger life of the general body. Thus, society in a state
of freedom, where alone there is growth, always develops from within. It is the quality and force of the
internal which creates the external, for power is at
the center. Society lives by the incessant reproduction
of the social elements, a generative process which has
for its end the perpetuation of the species, and consequently of society. There are two phases of reproduction, two complementary actions, the one internal and
the other external; it is like the kernel and the shell.
To accomplish its ends, sociology should be scientific,
with orderly classifications. Social phenomena are influenced by the external environment, which includes
the historic epoch, physiographic surroundings, and
ethnic inheritance, and by material and moral factors.

From all of this it can be seen that the Kingdom of
Heaven must fulfil all of the fundamental human
needs, and its perfection is the pattern and goal of all
social endeavor. In the spiritual world the government proceeds from the interiors of its organic structure, its purpose is the development and advancement
of all individuals, it conserves personal ability and
genius, adds to their values, and directs the perfected
and combined energies to the one end of preserving

and perpetuating its own order and structure. Those who cannot, because of their nature, be assimilated and introduced into its order and made a working part of it, are excluded and kept in a mere semblance of existence, where they can contribute indirectly to the general usefulness.

Genuine and constructive sociology rests on a psychologic understanding of the higher self, the spiritual man, and this has as a basis the biologic knowledge of structure and growth. The psychic and supernatural are important factors in the cosmo-sociologic order. No social organization could perpetuate itself unless some of its individuals were inspired by worthy ideals. The civic consciousness is an awareness of some noble goal within the reach of the community effort, and by attainment of which every individual is enriched. The difficulty facing human government is the lack of mutual agreement in adopting methods for ultimating its ideals.

Religious ideals have a binding force on conscience and behavior, and it is therefore essential that religious concepts have their sources in fundamental truths, and not in prejudices and mind-binding dogmas which have no authority save that of tradition. Unseeming as it may sound, one of the obstacles in the path of orderly government is the common religious mind. The mystic union, as the early religious leaders imagined it, was strictly confined to those on earth who were the designated followers of the Christ; it did not include the entire human race, pagan, Gentile and barbaric. In the real Kingdom of Heaven all human beings must find their place and work; it is true that those who have no ability or energy, or are incapable of adjustment, must be isolated. But, this exclusion is not based on beliefs, but on the will to live creatively.

In our world to-day there is a universal belief in God, but there is no common agreement in defining the personality and purpose of the Deity. Until there is a clearer understanding of the nature of the Divine, there can be no unity among men on a firm social basis. Every tribe, people, and nation has its concept of the Invisible Power, developed from some viewpoint that is traditional; only when these can be harmonized can we expect a rational understanding of the plan and purpose of human life, for that life is inevitably bound up with its Creator. In the Kingdom of Heaven the assimilation and allocation of incoming members must be natural and orderly, for good always survives its transitions. Evil always accomplishes its own decline and extinction, just as in the material world the parasitic and predacious destroy themselves.

Science has accomplished wonders in its explanation of the physical universe, and the Christian religion has contributed toward a better understanding among men of various nations, and thus assisted in the stabilization of political government, but the organized church has produced no new spiritual ideals since the time of the Christ. The mind of modern man, with its changed outlook on existence and the universe, revolutionary in many ways, craves a rational religion in keeping and harmony with its knowledge. The principles of that religion, from a sociologic standpoint, must be inspired by charity and brotherly love, and in which the rights and freedom of every individual in this world must be respected and protected. We cannot conceive religious belief as a fixed dogma; there must be an increasing spiritual enlargement and understanding which will be in step with the scientific age.

The religious spirit is inherent in man. It has native intuitions which express themselves according to the period and the existing level of culture. Religious experience is individual, it cannot be standardized. Man has always had a sense and feeling of dependence, for he is surrounded by forces which he does not fully understand, and not under his control. With these unknown powers and forces he longs to bring himself into harmony, and establish a relationship which intuition and practice force him to believe must be to mutual advantage. This extension of his mind into his world must produce evidences of satisfaction before he can seriously adjust himself to a definite social order. In the presence of this higher power he feels a sense of reverence, because he knows that it is superior to him, and like Moses before the burning bush, his naked feet must also touch the ground he stands on. He therefore regards the unknown as sacred, as having thoughts above his thoughts, and ways beyond his ways.

Man cannot deny the reality of the spiritual, he may call it mysterious, but he insists on some explanation and apprehension of his veiled surroundings, so that he may with reason enter into the superior plan and purpose. The keen desire for understanding above faith is the active factor in controlled behavior, and in the attempts at conforming ritualism. It is in this modern way that man has gradually changed his conception of God, and nothing save an exalted yet reasonable idea of the Divine will satisfy him to-day. Man has, through personal experience, discovered some truths of vital importance, and no religious system that omits these truths can appeal to him. Our bodies and minds have been molded into relationship with the world in which we find ourselves, and we know that the world is not of our own making, therefore relationship has purpose. That same relationship must prevail in the spiritual world if it is to complement and develop man. The religious spirit of man needs contact with the human side of the creator; and the religious spirit and the scientific spirit must combine efforts in this great experiment, for they both lead along the unbeaten path to the house of truth.

There are social implications in the teachings of Jesus which the theologians have never developed. His teachings, as stated by Matthew in recording the Sermon on the Mount, contain a social doctrine of great promise to those who seek fundamental principles, and these teachings have their primitive roots in the book of Deuteronomy, and the Law revealed to Moses. Because Jesus spoke to a more developed mind and age, he clarifies the principles and relates them to the common behavior of his day; and above all he emphasizes human values as superior to property rights. He could not proceed beyond enunciating the general principles and their application to social and individual behavior, because the specific technique for working them out is always the task of intelligent research and experiment in the particular age that adopts them. At his day the machinery was not at hand, and in the brevity of his days he confined himself to the adjustment of man to the Kingdom of Heaven.

Apostolic Christianity began with the effort to remold the social order. In its primitive membership there were no racial, class, or property distinctions. The experiment was defeated by the aristocratic converts, and the church abandoned the task of revolutionizing the social order of this world, and transferred the hope to a future world. Thus was the actual defeat of the social doctrine of Jesus accomplished. In the subsequent failure his predictions were verified, and his wisdom proved. We must recapture the original ideals of Jesus, which have an especial appeal since we have failed in other theories, and begin again to construct the social order so that men may be released from a bondage borne throughout the centuries. Let us grasp the pattern of the Kingdom of Heaven with a full understanding, for its structure will aid us, and as we build the inspiration of its members will flow into our efforts and guide our hands and minds.

That the actual recognized results of our present social order are in acute contradiction to the Christian conceptions of justice and brotherhood will be admitted by anyone who gives the matter serious thought. Fortunately, religion is more sane to-day; the discarded evangelism of the past sought to create a sense of fear and a conviction of sin and unworthiness, and these weaknesses defeat human purpose. The effort should be to emphasize social responsibilities, otherwise the denial of this aspect of religion as an expression of life leaves world experience without instructive meaning, and prevents spiritual incentive from finding a world basis. There is no occasion for the control of conduct if we have no goal in view that is higher than obedience to animal instincts. Sublimation of character, which is the effort to substitute a higher set of thoughts and ideals as a replacement for the lower, loses all meaning when we deny the spiritual nature of man a field for practical action.

The only excuse would be the herd instinct of sympathetic feeling for the material needs of the group or community. Any philosophy we accept must certainly fit into its own scheme and prove its own merits. Even the herd instinct has a metaphysical basis, for its tenure of existence presupposes the continued life of the herd. The Kingdom of Heaven, like the social systems of men, and like the cosmic universe, is a process of attaining instances of definite experience out of its own elements. The will to be has a psychic and religious incentive; it is an expression of the conscious power inherent in the spiritual constitution of man.

A satisfactory social order suitable for this world could not be formulated by present religious leaders from the material at their disposal, for they have a partial view only of the human realities. The incompleteness of religion is due to its attitude; it regards truth as something handed down from the past, which must be jealously guarded lest men violate its sanctity, and stray from its authority. The trend of Scripture, when correctly understood, is a sequence of constant development in which the principle of truth is apprehended and adjusted to the problems of each succeeding age. Science is an aspect of religion, for it is a constant progress toward truth of material manifestations, and this is essential, for we must first understand God in our own world before we can apprehend Him as He is in the spiritual world. The two worlds have an affinity, and one explains the other. For us on earth, the spiritual world is always a future vision, it does not reside in a fabled past.

The spirit of free inquiry, which is not necessarily to think unlike others, must be defended from assault by those who rest faith on authority. In the scientific pursuit, theories which supersede earlier ones are links in a long chain of progressive advances likely in time to be themselves transcended. Their only justification is their adequacy for the relevant facts. They are temporary resting-places in the search for truth; they are mental training methods, and there is nothing absolute about them. Religious truth is said to belong to heaven; this is an incomplete statement, for religious truth belongs to men in our world, else it would not have been revealed, and with us those truths are always provisional and tentative. If they cannot be worked out by men in this world, and prove their adequacy for human solution, then it is doubtful whether they can be applied with success in heaven.

Science demands induction from facts, and not deduction from dogmas. We must face our facts and derive our conclusions from them, and not start with the conclusions and then play with the facts. Reasoning in religion is mostly a rearrangement of our prejudices; often we claim a denominational faith because our fathers bore the same label. The modern temper insists that the scientific attitude of veracity and self-detachment must be applied in all human affairs. The common tendency of orthodox religion to mistake desires for facts, to assume a world to be what we should like it to be, to reserve a certain part of our interests as falling outside the scope of ordinary knowledge, is the direct opposite of empirical science.

The roots of all great thinking and noble living lie deep in the human soul itself, and not in the surface of rational comparisons; all creative work in science, philosophy and religion is inspired by intuitive experience in which other world forces are involved. Inspiration is not a heat or light that deprives us of our reason and then takes possession of us, it is not a substitute for thought, it is a challenge to the intelligence. The inspiration is operative throughout the entire process of the collection of facts, the brooding over them, the gradual grip of the tension, the sudden release and mastery of the elaboration of the concepts and judgments.

> Whereof all excellence upspringeth of itself,
>   Like a rare fruit upon some gifted stock ripening
> On its arch-personality of inborn faculty
>   Without which gift creative reason is barren.

The human mind is value-seeking; it strives for unity and coherence, for harmony and beauty, for worth and goodness, but we cannot place these in categories as realities by themselves. The spiritual consciousness is not reducible to either intellectual or esthetic activity, or the sum of these; it is an autonomous form of life which transcends all of these. The object of the spiritual mind is not either the true or the good, or the beautiful, or the mere unity of them, but a knowledge of the personality of God the universal consciousness, who includes all of these values in their divine realities. Truth, beauty and goodness do not exist outside of Him, and when the spiritual mind reacts to these forces it is responding to the divine inspiration, and expressing something inherent in the Creative Source.

When we tune in on the Kingdom of Heaven we discover these values in their highest perfection, and apprehend the method by which they are applied to actual heavenly conditions. We can understand the heavenly order because we find it natively human, the responses there are similar to the mental and physical responses that we have observed in our own minds and bodies. The light from heaven illuminates every process and action of this world, and creates in us an awareness of unlimited resources and unbounded possibilities. It stimulates the desire to be, it gives each individual a place in the divine scheme and plan, it explains our world and makes everything beautiful and worth while. The most humble task; the least noticed sacrifice, the silent tear, can become a dew-drop into which the heavenly light can shine and make it more radiant than a precious diamond. It helps the awakened individual to discriminate between information, fact and truth, and when he thus holds himself receptive of the truth he recognizes his obligation to his fellow-men, to give it out again after it is made richer and purer by his personal interpretation.

> Else whence this pleasing hope, this fond desire,
>   This longing after immortality?
>   Why shrinks the soul
>   Back on herself, and startles at destruction?
> 'Tis the divinity that stirs within us;
>   'Tis heaven itself that points out an hereafter
> And intimates eternity to man.

CHAPTER IX

FROM PHYSICAL TO SPIRITUAL REALITIES

As many ages as it took to form
The world, it takes to form the human race.
God plans; man works; God oversees the work.
The stately frame of the harmonic world
Rises even now, though men perceive it not.
From all the quarries of the earth are hewn
The stones of that vast fabric.

THE historic evolution of the human race shows con-clusively that there is a succession of human experi-ences. It is by methods of comparative experience that man has gained a knowledge of the cosmic universe and of his own nature. Man cannot be divorced from his world entirely, for at death he carries the rudiments of his acquired cosmic knowledge with him to the world of spiritual reality. What he has seen and experienced here becomes the basis of his understanding of the Kingdom of Heaven, for the external environment is remarkably similar, and disabuses the mind at once of any sense of unfitness or alienation.

The fact that science and religion are agreed that there is a creative coördination is sufficient ground for postulating a spiritual world. When thrilled by the beauty of a physical phenomenon, the beholder has many questions to ask. There are questions unanswered when we contemplate the spiritual world. What is love? How does it create and impart power? How does it mold and temper everything to its adaptations? What is the substance of truth? How does it enter and animate the human mind? When a furnace radiates heat it sets countless molecules into motion, and collisions ensue which create chaos, but on closer examination this seeming chaos resolves itself into dynamic order.

When we see the variety of human reactions, and recognize that no two persons are alike in temperament or disposition, we wonder how this flow of diverse characteristics can be coördinated in the orderly concourse of the Kingdom of Heaven, and be made to register in constructive ways its creative powers. What heat is to scientific understanding, love is to spiritual understanding. When heat is accelerated it is transformed into light; in like manner when love is released in created channels it takes on the form of truth. Truth is love in creative action, and love is undeveloped truth, and these two substances are the energies of the Kingdom of Heaven. By means of their equilibrium experimental chaos is transformed into spiritual order and structure. Just as the objects of the physical world are made up of atoms of various electric centers, so are the structures of the spiritual world formed of truths and loves of various energies and proportions. The spiritual world is just as scientific in principle as is the cosmic universe.

Therefore a knowledge of the future life and of the Kingdom of Heaven clarifies thought and purpose, encourages practical effort, develops personal responsibility, and helps the individual to recognize his place in the orderly scheme of life. The Kingdom of Heaven is not a mystic unreality. Its order and function can be apprehended rationally, for its modes do not violate our knowledge of coördination as we have seen its operation in this world. The Kingdom of Heaven is an organic unity, which serves a supreme purpose, and completes the circle of life; it is not a realm of limited existence. The human experiences of earth-life have been a preparation for more sublime experiences.

Those who come to the Kingdom of Heaven either in this world or after death discard many of the impressions which belong solely to the physical sensations, and adjust themselves to a new environment. This is possible because latent spiritual talents have arrived at the threshold of a realm for which they have been in preparation from birth. Spiritual knowledge that has been developed through a series of experiences becomes the measure of our mental capacity. There is consequently a reversal of values, the worldly unsuccessful may become the spiritual leaders, and the world's heroes often shrink in dimension and gravitate to the bottom of the scale. That which is loved to the exclusion of all else becomes the dominating passion, and if this love can serve a use in the Kingdom of Heaven it intuitively discovers its place and function. There are no arbitrary decisions or unreasonable distinctions, there are no grants to personal favor, no choice of self-interest. Those who coveted the high places may be demoted to the lowest, and those who in humility sought insignificant rôles may be elevated to superior functions. Every individual is what he has been, spiritually. "Unto him that hath (spiritual capacities) shall be given, and from him that hath not shall be taken that which he hath."

No doubt this new classification is the most startling phenomenon of the spiritual world. The entire aspect of life is revolutionized, self-interest is suppressed and discarded, and spiritual motives which seek serviceable action are released. What was considered of small value in the physical world assumes miraculously inestimable proportions. Under the new impulse the individual finds himself, and is stirred to attain results impossible before this incentive was felt. This realization may be startling to some, but to the individual who can respond, it is a release of repressed resources; it is the triumph of spirit over matter. The changed conditions awaken an entirely new set of reactions, the response is to spiritual impulsions, and their apprehension is limited only by the personal understanding of truth and the measure of affection for community service. The abilities which were directed to accumulate wealth, or to attain worldly distinction, find no material on which to work; they are useless tools in the new world. Motives which developed along lines of unselfish work, professions which demanded personal sacrifice, affections that sought expression in community welfare, all of these will find a new field and satisfaction that surpass any sensation known to the physical body. Therefore, it is not what we do in the world of nature, but the spirit in which it is done. It is the essence of the professional or manual service we are engaged in, and not the shell, which makes for character and spiritual adaptation. The Kingdom of Heaven needs those who have given a drink of water to the thirsty, shelter to the homeless, ministration to the sick, and those in prison, for this is the essence of charity. The thirsty and homeless are those who are craving for truth, and the sick folk and bound are those who are hereditarily and emotionally unadjusted. The selections made in the world of spirit depend upon the grade of developed capacity, and the law operates in orderly fashion so that of two grinding at a mill, one shall be taken and the other left; of those in the fields some shall be called and others rejected. Truth will be separated from its accompanying falsities and illusions, and love will be purified and released from its perversions and adulterants. The pure affections and the true knowledges will be coördinated and form the central core of personality. Thus at the very entrance of the spiritual world every individual is examined, internally adjusted, and spiritually instructed, all of which preserves the order and purpose of the Kingdom of Heaven.

Nothing can be organized unless the parts are in agreement and each fulfils its allotted function. This principle is amply demonstrated in the physical world, in the human body and mind, in every department of the universe. The spiritual world is a society or community of human beings. It is composed of those who have mutual relationships founded on a spiritual basis. Its parts are aggregations of human beings who have ascended the scale of spiritual realizations and are agreed on a common purpose. Its groups, depending upon their apprehension of truth and technical expression of affection, are distinct from each other; each has its special quality. Distance is not spacial, it is according to states of mind and affectional interests. In the Father's house there are many mansions, because the nature of man is preserved in its varieties. Running through Greek philosophy and Victorian poetry is the constantly recurring idea that life divides itself into many parts and each particle reflects some aspect of the infinity of life.

In the organic universe there will be chaos unless its units are guided by an inherent power of coördination. The organic, like the inorganic universe, has its microcosm, and the fundamental units continually absorb food and manufacture energies which are utilized for coördinated creative processes. Chemical activities also are chaotic as caloric activities until coördinated, although the structure of this coördinator is unknown to science. Everything grows and multiplies in orderly fashion at the expense of specific energies in creative coördination, because it transforms chaos into functioning structures. In every known case the object of coördination is to ascend to a higher plane in the scheme of life by rendering a superior service. Science cannot begin to describe the creative process without using terms which are applicable to the structure of the internal spiritual world. It hesitates in drawing spiritual conclusions while at the same time holding to material fact, as Tennyson has well expressed:

> I hold thee here, root and all, in my hand
> Little flower—but if I could understand
> What you are, root and all, and all in all,
> I should know what God and man is.

The groups in the Kingdom of Heaven are distinguished by the intensity of their emotions and their understanding of truth. Emotion is the spiritual energy which corresponds to material heat, and intelligence is the spiritual counterpart of light. Sadi Carnot originally formulated the principle that heat, to render service, must be guided in its passage from higher to lower temperatures. When this energy is not guided it is wasted. Speculative physics, which has awakened recently in its approach to the problems concerned in heat and light, may discover from spiritual laws that heat is the cohesion of atoms attracted by a retarded center, and light is atomic speed or released heat. In the spiritual world the varieties of emotional temperature produce a power when guided and coördinated, and the passage of heat or emotion, from group to group, creates light or intelligence. If we carry Carnot's principle to its spiritual implications we may conclude that he is as much a prophet as a physicist.

In Maxwell's formulation of the fundamental laws of electric motions the principle is, that light is an activity of electric forces, generated in the interior of luminous bodies. In the starlit vault of the heavens is the inspiration which made the Psalmist exclaim, "The firmament showeth his handiwork." The motion of the planets and of other material bodies in the heavens as well as on earth is the result of an ideal coördination in which material bodies of one type of temperature act on bodies of a different degree. The variety in temperature displayed by the stars furnishes an illustration of the degrees of emotion in the groups of the Kingdom of Heaven. Michael Pupin, commenting on this harmony, says, "A more complete analysis of the beauty of law and order in the coördinated physical world was never given by mortal man."

There is a cosmic stream of solar energy from which everything in our planet derives its driving force. By its power vaporous water-masses are carried from the earth to high elevations, in descending, each drop performs a mission, purifying, cleansing, refreshing everything in its path, until it returns to the bosom of its mother-ocean. In spiritualizing this concept the poet could describe in adequate language the power of love to elevate truth, suspend it over the anxious minds of men, and then release it so that it may descend into the several planes of thought, cleansing and refreshing every channel of the mind, so that it may flow down the streams of human activities and settle in the institutional forms of community service. Thus is truth in its cycle the illuminating energy of the ages.

There is a law of association. In our world people find those congenial who have similar interests and who are harmonious in their viewpoints; in the spiritual world groups are conjoined, not by necessity, but because of like genius and similarity of affection and mental persuasion. If changes occur they are caused by states of mind and affection of pursuit. Every chemist knows that each cell is a microcosm consisting of vast numbers of units, working alongside each other and having a common goal in view. This goal is the development of superior forms of cells constructed to accomplish definite functions. Their structures are carefully adjusted with reference to their functions, and in this manner caloric and chemical energies are transformed from chaos to coördinated and orderly structures.

Each autonomous organic structure, the organic body, is a macrocosm, an aggregation of cellular microcosms, which displays the same coördinated activity observable in the fundamental units. Thus does nature supply information on the laws of the spiritual world, for the same principle is active in the Kingdom of Heaven, where each individual, after a course of training in the material world, finds his place, his companions and his function. Companionship is according to the nature of the affection and the ability for performing duties.

When the spirit of man is released from the body at death, it preserves its human form of knowledge and love, for as Saint Paul said, "There is a spiritual body and there is a natural body." The mental vision is then freed from many handicaps, and from those grosser matters which occupied it in the world. Thought is clarified to a marvelous degree; it is accelerated and synchronized with the tempo of the spiritual world. Perceptions, intuitions and moods, and conviction of truth, are wonderfully expressed without the use of language, but by the eyes, the expressions of the face and the surrounding sphere. Thoughts are audible in rhythmic music, and visible in gorgeous colors, and this transformation is spontaneous and free of mechanisms. In our world, due to scientific discovery, we are approaching the fringe of the spiritual laws in the use of the radio and the perfecting of television. Sound and color are elementary and complementary expressions of heat and light, and heat and light are material correlatives of spiritual love and truth. The laws of the material and of the spiritual worlds have a common denominator; science and religion are the two faculties used in the discovery of truth.

External Appearance of the Other World

From the human viewpoint the appearance of the spiritual world, in general, is very much like that of the material world, so much so, that those who make the safe passage scarcely know that they are in another world. This general similarity makes the exit from our world very pleasing, and assists the spirit in accommodating itself to its surroundings. The substances of that world are spiritual, yet they are real and actual to the sight of the spirit. The physical universe cannot appear to the sight of the spirit after the optic nerve is paralyzed or dissolved, for the spiritual eye can see only those things which are spirit in substance. This fact will explain how and why Miss Helen Keller, who is physically blind and deaf, can tell us, "The only really blind are those who will not see the truth—those who shut their eyes to the spiritual vision. For them alone darkness is irrevocable. Those who explore the dark with love as a torch, and truth as a guide, find it good. Blind people who have eyes know that they live in a spiritual world inconceivably more wonderful than the material world that is veiled from them. The landscapes they behold never fade; the flowers they look upon are the immortal flowers which bloom in God's garden. These abundant truths are for those who hunger and thirst in their pilgrimage through an age of materialism. I have walked through its sunlit ways of truth, I have drunk of its sweet waters of knowledge, and the eyes of my spirit have been opened, so that I know the joy of vision which conquers darkness and circles heaven. I bury my fingers in this great river of light that is higher than all stars, deeper than the silence which enfolds me. It is also a fact that that world presents a system of perfect order, and every part of it fits into every other part. The same laws apply to the constitution of the spiritual realm, the spiritual interpretation of the Bible, and the mind of man. Most human minds are so constituted that there is in them a secret chamber where religious subjects are stored, and their center is the idea of God. If the idea is false and cruel, all things which follow it by logical sequence partake of these qualities. For the highest is also the inmost, and it is the essence of every belief and thought and institution derived from it. This essence, like the soul, forms into an image of itself everything it enters; and as it descends to the planes of daily action, it lays hold of the truths in the mind and infects them with its cruelty and error."

For those who endure the pressure of the soul against the prison-bars of flesh, these words spoken from the soul of Miss Keller give a reassuring nearness which will relieve the intelligence and lighten the burden of every man and woman in the world. It helps us to recognize that in the Kingdom of Heaven the surroundings are not composed of material matter, and it is not a fixed environment such as we have in this world. It is flexible and vibrant, responsive to the sphere of emotion and thought radiating constantly from the group of persons occupying it. It is in continuous motion and in the perpetual act of re-creation. The environment has also an added quality, for there is a constant influx of the general tone and temper of the coördinated heavens. There is therefore an agreement between the objective spiritual world and the interior states of the individuals in the group. The latter creates the former, and the one reacts to the other. This principle of harmony is fundamental, and gives intensity and quality to the group, and aids in distinguishing the one group from the others. This fact of external environment agreeing with internal state can be observed by those who analyze their moods and experiences. To the gloomy, depressed and despairing man the whole world takes on an indigo tint corresponding to his mood, and he sees everything as hostile to his success. There are also rose-tinted glasses for those who in our world are optimistic and adventurous.

> Spirit ay shapeth matter into view,
> As music wears the forms it passes through,
> Spirit is lord of substance, matter's sole
> First cause and forming power and final goal.

To him who can imagine what this harmony between internal state and external fact can produce there comes a vision of the glory and beauty which must surround those in the Kingdom of Heaven who are adjusted to its rhythm. We recall David Grayson's words, "We forget that there are five chords in the great scale of life—sight, hearing, smell, taste, touch—and few of us ever master the chords well enough to get the full symphony of life, but are like children playing Peter Piper with one finger while all the music of the universe is in the Great Instrument, and all to be had for the taking." Our earthly limitations may prevent enjoyment of the physical world, but in the spiritual world

these barriers are removed and there is a complementary emotion which accompanies the released creative energies and faculties. Human language is barren
of words and symbols capable of describing the scenery
of the other world; musical composers and poets have
often attempted it, perhaps color-artists and perfume-
specialists can contribute to the effort.

The spiritual objects, while real and substantial, are
in constant motion which produces changes, for they
express the internal thought and love of those who
dwell in them. The garments of the individuals have a
tint and color-shade corresponding to the spiritual
state of the wearer; thus the persons within the group
are distinguishable by their dress, for conscious personality is never lost even in the largest groups. The principle and quality of the internal nature is harmoniously
objectified, the house and garden are in agreement
with the occupant, for the surroundings take on the
various hues, forms and fragrances that best express
the state of mind and feeling. Even from our present
human experience we know that mental and emotional
states are always in flux, and no existence is so firmly
fixed or somber that it does not have its relaxations
and alternations. Man's experience in the spiritual
world follows the same laws which are feebly expressed
and scarcely understood in the external natural world.
Each group in the Kingdom of Heaven fixes its own
environment, and the combined effect of all the groups
expresses the fullness of infinite life. It is the grand
symphony of heaven, and surpasses in glory the most
elaborate dreams of anyone on our earth.

The Coördinated Groupings of the Other World

Social consciousness began when men first recognized that the individual is only a part of the complex

community, in which the large numbers of autonomous individuals are in pursuit of the same objective, self-existence and self-expression. To guide this complex effort to an orderly system, so that it might escape extinction and avoid the threatened chaos, became the problem that required solution, and out of this quest has come the evolution of human government. As a first step to the solution it becomes necessary for man to find himself, and discover those points of contact that make him one with those of his kind. For this reason we cannot begin to know ourselves unless we understand that there are qualities within each of us which survive death. Only then can we have perfect communion in acting and thinking as though we were immortal, and thus cultivating the unlimited areas yet to be realized. We find ourselves gradually and eventually, and what is true of the individual is also true of human society in its evolution. We are continually in the act of perfecting, yet never absolutely perfect. Life unfolds like a green bud, it flowers and blooms, the petals wither and fall and the fragrance escapes, only to reveal the fruit yet to be ripened, and in the kernel of that seed is still the norm and gene of a prolonged existence.

There are reasons why no formula, no precise statement of data can be supplied, for we are always in the making. Our one guide is the immediate contact with spiritual realities, for these carry us on to the ultimations which are at present unknown to us.

> We are in very truth that which we love;
> And love, like noblest deeds, is born of faith.

When we look into the organic system of the human body we see that all parts are arranged according to their use and function. Each cell finds the place where it can be of maximum service. The same principle of action prevails in the organic human mind, although here the will of the individual determines the arrangement. We would be wanting in logic and reason if we did not conjecture that the same order is observed in the organic form of the Kingdom of Heaven. Its order is derived from the mutual love and service, for each individual in his every thought and movement regards the welfare of the organization as of prime importance. Each member therefore communicates his delight to others, and the larger the numbers the more evident and intense is the rapture arising from the mutual harmony. The resulting sphere is radiated by degrees, more ecstatic with those who are sensitive to its vibrations, and diminishing as it extends to the less responsive, and thus an equilibrium is maintained. This is true because each individual is in a sense passive, and responding according to his internal nature to the communicated sphere. The joy is increased and becomes more perfect in its operation as numbers of individuals are contacted and participate in the communion.

The Kingdom of Heaven is formed of societies and communities which have inter-relationships something like the systems of the human body, for the body gives its modes of expression to the spirit of man, and at the same time supplies the mind of man with impressions from the external world. The action is complementary both in the body and the spiritual world. The societies of the Kingdom of Heaven have a wider range, for they are more compact and perfect; they have as an objective the welfare of the entire human family in both worlds, and thus give to life its most perfect expression. The cells and organs of the human body unconsciously direct their energies to one purpose, but the society action of the Kingdom of Heaven is a conscious operation, it is intelligent and sensitive to all its reactions and every form of resistance. The relationship is therefore not only to its parts, but to every action in the whole realm of human relations. This coordination is so specific that there are spiritual functions which correspond to the operations of the isthmus of the brain, the nerves and glands from which proceed the fibers that inspire and direct the various functions of the physical body.

In the human brain there are circumvolutions and foldings within which are the cortical substances. From these, fibers proceed that constitute the medulla. They extend thence through the nerves into the many parts of the body. Thus the body is at the control of the brain, and everything of the body is governed by the mind by means of the brain. There is a central seat of government with its many concordant parts. From this organization in the body of man some idea may be gained of the arrangement of the Kingdom of Heaven. All of its societies and groups are controlled on the same principle, they are coördinated as to functions, receiving and giving to each other, in a wonderful community of interests. All are free and independent, and no two alike, yet held compactly together under the central control. There is a gyrating movement and a continuous flow, of which the single individual is not aware, and the organism is never at absolute rest.

While the atomic and molecular activity of our stellar system is not a cosmos, but is a dynamic chaos, yet there is an order in the movement of each planet around its center, and of each solar system in its orbital movement around some distant point. The speed of the universe is beyond calculation, yet no person on our planet feels the slightest vibration. We may learn from these scientific facts something of the truth of the realities of the other world. Science tells us of the orbit of our planet around the sun, and the resultant recurrence of the terrestrial seasons are known to us. They succeed each other with a rhythm which has not changed perceptibly within historic records, and this unchangeable law of action between material bodies may grant us some knowledge of the vibrations of the spiritual bodies.

Because of the similarity of form which exists in the human body and in the Kingdom of Heaven, a mode of descent and ascent is effected and maintained between the two. The descent is through man into the world, and ascent from mineral, vegetable, and animal, through man into the spiritual world. The precision and perfection of this operation is beyond comprehension.

The terraqueous globe is a matrix from which are produced the effects that are the ultimates of nature. The creative process is beautifully exhibited in the evolution of matter, for this is still an infant universe in its swaddling clothes. The objects on earth are an image, more or less perfect, of co-related things in the spiritual world. The extending spheres, which are spiritual at their source, become the active principle in the receptive forms of material things, in seeds and soils, and are the causal forces of the material energies of this world. These radiating spheres are not physical or material, but they make contact at the most sensitive point with material, just as the mind makes contact with the brain, and the soul with the body. In nature everything has a granular structure, the granules of matter are atoms and molecules, the granules of electricity are the positive and negative electrons. The granules of organic life are the microscopic cells and their millions of constituent parts. The thought might

be carried on to the nation, where the granules are the
millions of human citizens. The full meaning of organic
life is still a mystery, but the physical foundation of life
is yielding to the penetrating mind of man. The beauty
of its material structure, and its operations, can be apprehended from the point of view of dynamics of non-
coördination. Every vegetable and mineral, as well as
man, is within the scope of the extending spheres of the
spiritual world.

These spheres activate and awaken the potential
faculties within the person, and then add something
from themselves. In writing a book, the author types
word after word to convey his thought to the reader,
because language is an accepted medium utilized by the
mind for its expression. In like manner the emanating
sphere of the spiritual world uses those forms of matter
through which its power of generation can be made
manifest. Nothing can exist or subsist from itself, it is
kept true to form by the force that is prior to it. There
is a continual contact of the spiritual world with the
natural world, and in the operation material forms
are directed to their uses by the reactions they give to
the impinging spiritual incentive. The contact of
spiritual with physical is in the use and service, and not
with matter or form. Elemental material substances
are not simple; they contain within themselves great
possibilities, and these are developed by spiritual initia-
tive to meet the demands of other substances which
they can serve. Seeds have within themselves anterior
primitive forms derived from the mineral kingdom
that emerge in higher uses. Molecules are composed
of atoms, atoms of electrons, and within that the hypo-
thetical sub-electronic world, vanishing to the unrealized. The pageantry of evolution exhibits the work of
the spiritual spark active in the world of matter.

To know—
Rather consists in opening out a way
Whence the imprisoned splendor may escape,
Than in effecting entry for a light
Supposed to be without.

Without the spiritual, observe,
The natural's impossible;—no form,
No motion, without sensuous, spiritual
Is inappreciable;—no beauty or power.

The generative power in the things of nature, and in
the intelligence, knowledge, and wisdom of man, are
from the spiritual world; therefore both man and
matter have an inclination for service, and the sensation
in man is that of conscious delight. When the form is
dissolved, the spiritual persists and discovers other
means of manifestation.

Relation between Internal and External

Man has a dual nature; he has spiritual obligations
and physical responsibilities. This duality is indicated
in his body. There are right and left lobes of the
brain, two divisions of the heart and lungs, two arms
and limbs, two eyes and ears, and these external parts
correspond to internal capacities which are two-fold,
the will and its emotions and the understanding with its
thoughts. There is an external and an internal in all
things and all operations. The human mind recognizes
both sides of a question, and its variations are due to
the shifting from one side to the other, but as the mind
becomes more perfect in the other world it has a purer
perception of truth, and the sensations arising from this
knowledge are sublime in a degree that cannot be described. In our world the human mind operates largely
on its lower levels because man is engaged in the dis-

covery of the secrets of nature, its phenomena, and the principles and laws of its order. If this choice were not granted the human race would not advance in knowledge, and men would not desire to be wiser than others.

There is a constant relation between a man's motives and his actions, and between the thoughts of his mind and the feelings of his spirit. The human mind is the conscious side of the soul or spirit, and when a person passes to the other world the spirit becomes conscious of its personality, and the lower levels of the mind become unconscious because they have no material thoughts to engage them. There are two forces which keep all things in their connection and order, one force acting on the internal and the other on the external, and thus all things are kept in equilibrium.

When we turn to the scientific aspect of the universe let us remember that no scientist claims to have a complete picture of the creative process, but there are sufficient facts to demonstrate the principle on which the contact is made between the visible and the invisible. In examining vegetable forms we find that they receive the non-coördinated radiant energy of the sun and transform the energy of the celestial chaos into coördinated terrestrial service, and without this service there would soon be an end to all earthly life. The response which the seed and plant make to the sunlight is not from the sun, but has its source in the spiritual world.

The radiant energy of the sun comes to this planet as electric waves. Mathematics tells us that this energy is received and converted by material structures because their molecular elements resonate electrically to the particular wave-length agreeable to them. When the reactions of planetary atoms are in harmony with the transmitted waves of the solar atoms there is a sympathetic responsiveness. This harmony which exists between planetary bodies is the principle of relationship evident not only in nature, but also in the spiritual world, and between what is material and what is spiritual.

There is beyond doubt in the universe a pure atom which will some day be discovered by science, that will explain the relationship and the nature of light and heat. It seems that light is the result of the maximum speed of this pure atom, and heat is the minimum of its speed. The physicists assure us that the components of atomic structure are an equal number of positive and negative electrons; the positive electrons cohere at the point of the central positive nucleus when attracted by a given number of negative electrons. There is an orbital movement of the remaining negative electrons around the central nucleus of the atom, and this is supposed to represent in microscopic form the structure of the solar system; it is a cosmos created by the law of internal and external relations. We find then that the law of the least form is the same law as that of the greatest form. Heaven and earth are linked together in marvelous ways, and the bond of union can be observed in every part.

In the human being this same law prevails; the energy flowing from the Kingdom of Heaven, when received and converted by man into coördinated service, reveals itself in his sensations and delights, physical actions and gestures, looks and speech. We become in a sense that which we love, and if the loves are pure and disinterested the face of the individual reflects his affections. Evil dispositions may change the features into animal expressions.

Strictly speaking, the flow of energy from the spiritual world is not into the receptive material form, for the material can never become spiritual, it is not continuous, but contiguous. The material operation begins when the material reacts to the impulsions of the spiritual, and the material responds in the degree that its organism is capable of executing its stimulated energy. Man differs from all other creatures in that his love and thought seek spiritual expression in the physical world. The soul of man is spiritual, and this is true of no other creature or object in our world.

The spiritual stimulations are limited by the capacity of execution within the receptive form. If these forms and substances are unorganized and gross, very little reaction is possible. Men who concentrate their thought and affection on worldly things seldom feel the spiritual stimulations, and do not recognize the superior power. Poets, scientists, musicians, and those who labor unselfishly in the pursuit of truth often feel the spiritual impact as inspiration, and people speak of it as genius. The materially minded man interferes with his spiritual contacts by placing handicaps in its path. Grief, discontent, anxiety, acquisitiveness and secretiveness hinder the operation. When ambitious and proud men desire to rule others, and seek to have them serve them, their capacities of reception are diminished, and thus self-seeking always defeats itself. Spiritual energy cannot be misused for individual gain, for it has the welfare of all humanity as its objective. The endeavor of the spiritual sphere is to make men more perfect, reliable, and useful, and to bring them into harmony with the creative energy, so that the created world beneath can be developed and released for the human welfare. Inherently man desires to be useful, and fears separation from the stream of spiritual power, and it is this unconscious fear that urges him to have and to hold life.

Every microscopic cell, and each system of the human body, is related to some part of the Kingdom of Heaven, and they act and react on each other in the common effort to be of service. This operation constantly renews the physical, for it is the process of creation. Modern psychology is analyzing sex-attraction, but it has not discovered that this attraction is from spiritual sources which generate and procreate uses. Therefore, in the creative plan, each sex feels incomplete, and the personality of a man needs a feminine partner of complementary mind and interests. Psychiatry studies the abuses of sex and attempts to cure them, but the permanent solution is in ultimating the spiritual effort, and the production of children.

Simple and innocent people of faith, who are not too proud to rely on Providence, and are of a charitable disposition, are often closer to the interior spheres of the spiritual world than those intellectuals who will not believe anything that cannot be proved by sense perception. When these latter come into the other world they are stupid and insensible, because the basis of their beliefs is destroyed. The learned in literature and the professions, regardless of their beliefs, often perform services in indirect ways, even when seeking distinction and honor, for the plan of life is so comprehensive that it can utilize every form of service and adapt it to its own purposes.

The relation between the societies of the Kingdom of Heaven and the organic systems of the human body and mind is not one of resemblance of form or parts, but a relation of functional operations. There is no function possible without its organized form, and it is the relationship of function and use that contacts the two worlds. It can now be known why and how man is an image, a microcosm, of the Kingdom of Heaven,

which is the macrocosm; and how the material world
at large is a physical image of lesser perfection of the
external spiritual world. The law of relation between
that which is internal with that which is external is
universal, it holds all things and all energies in contact, not only does it prevail in the whole, but in every
least part. We cannot escape the conclusion that life
has mastered its purposes.

> Life is a symphony divine:
>   Thy note is given to thee!
> And every note hath its own work
>   In the great harmony.

> The sun that draws the circling worlds
>   Sounds its appointed tone:
> Nor less hath ev'n the lowliest leaf
>   A note that is its own.

> Perhaps the jarring task that seems
>   A discord unto thee,
> Resolves the living strain of Life
>   Into some higher key.

The Three Planes of Life

An interesting study, which needs further development, is in observing the phenomena of life as they
affect various structures, and the type of response that
each structure makes to the impulsions of life. We
recognize life's continuous tendency to initiate action,
and must concede, contrary to philosophic speculation,
that the impulsion is with deliberate purpose. This
knowledge of result must be granted because we have,
at the end of motion, coördination and not chaos. The
idea of degrees or planes enters into ancient formulated thought. It is evident in everything of nature; its
concepts are in the science of geometry, and no vehicle

through which truth is stated can avoid its implications. There are degrees which are discrete, and each discrete degree has its individual continuous degrees. In nature there are the mineral, the vegetable, and the animal structures, and each of these has its grades and varieties. In man there is a physical plane, a mental-emotional plane, and a spiritual plane, and each of these has its variations from finer to grosser, from internal to external, from sensitive to insensitive and unconscious.

The three degrees in man have their origin in the spiritual world, and man is an image of that world. There are degrees of height similar to degrees of love. These degrees begin from interior principles and extend to the farthest externals, and the three degrees of love differ in structure and principle. They form the three planes of the Kingdom of Heaven. These degrees are generated one from the other, but they are not similar in substance or in effect. Something of this knowledge can be recognized in the actions of a human being. The center and core of man is love, this is his motivating principle; love creates the affection for thought, and thought creates ideas which have in them the desire for ultimation in deeds and works. The visible creations of man, his deeds and works are on a distinct plane, and the works are of many varieties. The thoughts of man are on a plane distinct from his works, and these thoughts and ideas are of infinite variety. The love of man, his emotional will, is distinct from his thoughts, and this plane of love has its infinite varieties; in fact, every individual is a form of love, and there are as many varieties as there are human beings.

Man's animal nature is his ultimate degree. It is the basic foundation of his activities, and is essential to

the development of his thoughts and love. All operations of the physical body are in three degrees; all
things of nature are according to three degrees; and
all things, civil, moral, and spiritual, advance and are
definable in three degrees. This fundamental principle
governs all things in the world, and prevails in the
Kingdom of Heaven.

Creation is perpetual because it begins from an internal principle of life, and as it descends it assumes
or forms external structures that are receptive of it.
Whatever man makes is artificial and lifeless, because
it has no internal re-creating principle. The works of
nature are wonderful, and more so when examined
under a microscope or telescope, because the life principle is manifested in them and they are in perpetual
creativeness. The difference can be seen when we observe a natural flower and compare it with the artificial imitation made of cloth, wax, or glass.

The degrees of breadth, which are similar to the
degrees of truth, are parallel to the degrees of love.
The higher degrees of truth are potential in man, and
they do not reach visibility until he comes into the
Kingdom of Heaven. The highest degrees of truth
cannot be stated in words or symbols, they do not
become articulate in this world except in the souls of
things, and these truths are dimly apprehended by
meditative perception. Truth has qualities that are real
and substantial, and these take on objective spiritual
form in the other world. Maeterlinck, an artist who
symbolized truths in the garments of imagery, tells in
The Blue Bird, how the Fairy gives to Tyltyl a magic
hat, having on it "the diamond that makes people see."
By the use of this hat and diamond, the various things
which surround the children, attend and serve them,
suddenly emit their souls and become alive. To those

who understand Maeterlinck, this diamond is the symbol of spiritual light or truth. It is the same light of which Tennyson speaks as "the light that never was on land nor sea." Diamonds are formed of carbon under tremendous pressures of heat, and those who delight in symbolism can follow the thought that truth is at its best when it is compelled by pure love, and they will know that heat is related to love, and carbon to natural knowledge. Therefore Tyltyl is told, "When you've got on the hat you turn the diamond a little . . . and it presses a bump which nobody knows of, and which opens your eyes. You can see at once inside of things. One little turn more and you behold the past; another little turn and you behold the future."

In defining the degrees of height and depth, the fact should be kept in mind that the operation is from interiors to externals, and from greatest to least. The three degrees differ in substance and form, for they are three separate planes. There are three degrees in all things of nature, and there are three degrees in all things spiritual; men on earth function on three planes, and when the individual passes to the other world there are three degrees opened to him which have been potential while he had the physical body. Because man has this potential ability of function, he can be elevated to the spiritual world after death of the body.

All created things are an image and symbol illustrating, each in its method, the grand purpose of life. Every mineral is at the bars ready to be released so that it may be of service to the world. Many of them form compounds and struggle upward through the plants. Vegetable seeds sink into soil and muck, spreading their roots deep into the soil, and absorb the mineral elements. Lifting upward their stems and branches so that they may discover the light and bathe in the moisture, they breathe in the carbon dioxide and throw out the oxygen, thus creating food and health-giving air for man. The constant and impelling urge of all things is to perform a service and to elevate structural forms so that they may, through them, find a path back to the source of things, to life itself. Structures of animal forms are on an ascending scale, from the simple, single-celled to the complex organisms of mammals, and every form has some relation to the mental and emotional qualities of man.

Generally speaking, the world outside man is an image of the world inside of man. This may be a cryptic or epigrammatic statement, but its truth has illustrations all along the line of physical and mental evolution. Trees in their structure and use, and all vegetable plants, have a relation to ideas and thoughts which develop just like seeds and finally produce fruit. This idea, just like a plant, has possibilities of enlargement and growth. Animals and animal forms, from the simplest to the most complex, have a symbolic relationship to human loves and affections, and their uses are co-related, and one aids us in understanding the other. Without the presence of animals and vegetables or plants in the world, the education of man and his mental development would be impossible.

> In observing mountains, plains and valleys,
>   Covered over to the deepest of the sea
> With the corals, grasses, grains and forests
>   Beautiful—Is that all they mean to me?
>
> I have learned that all minutest substance
>   Swung from infinitude into time and space,
> Is reflecting its Creator's wisdom—
>   That the world of matter is the spirit's base.

Nature's outer form is but a vessel
  In which the depths of inner meaning lie;
They reveal to me the living spirit,
  Speak a hidden language that can never die.

CHAPTER X

THE KINGDOM DEVELOPS

I have seen the Vision Beautiful;
  How human love can give
Its all, its best, to other souls
  And find it joy to live.
How, after windows opened wide
  Toward the heavenly air,
One day they find life glorified
  Beyond their every prayer.

IF ANY attempt were made to describe in detail the conditions prevailing at this day in the Kingdom of Heaven, the author would be compelled to descend to the realm of speculation, and that method is foreign to the purpose of this book. There are those who claim to have had a vision of that world, and any one not having shared in the experience is incompetent to deny the truth of their statements. There are many possibilities beyond the knowledge of individuals, less fortunately placed, but we can challenge the accuracy of their descriptions if they do not appear reasonably apparent in the light of our knowledge of cosmic law and human relations. Any world condition beyond us which does not accord with human reason, or harmonize with the mental and emotional reactions with which we are familiar, would be of little interest. If individual consciousness and personality are not preserved in the change from one world to the other, then you and I are out of the picture.

Scientific investigation during the past 150 years has gone deeply into the knowledge of the nature of matter, and we have facts at our command which were unknown to former generations, therefore we have now a reasonable basis of fundamentals upon which to interpret the higher implications of life. Scientific knowledge is advanced by volitionally postulating the unknown and probable, and then testing everything in the light of that assumption. Human thought has and must employ the same method in finding the pathway that leads to the future. In this technique it is often necessary to invent a new vocabulary to avoid difficulties of terms and description. Philosophy, science, religion, psychology, and modern mechanics labor under this disadvantage and must overcome the handicap before they can speak intelligibly.

Viewing life as we see it in action, we cannot deny that the spiritual is in close contact with the material. Thomas Carlyle, in *Sartor Resartus*, says, "All things visible are emblems; what thou seest is not there on its own account—strictly taken, it is not there at all. Matter exists only spiritually, and to represent some idea, and body it forth." Tennyson tells us that the spiritual is "nearer than hands and feet, closer than breathing." In *The Ancient Sage* we read of his experience,

> More than once when I sat alone
>   revolving in myself
> The word that is the symbol of myself,
> The mortal limit of the self was loosed
> And passed into the nameless as a cloud
> Melts into heaven, I touched my limbs, the limbs
> Were strange, not mine, and yet no shade of doubt,
> But utter clearness, and thro' loss of self
> The gain of such large life as match'd with ours
> Were sun to spark, unshadowable in words,
> Themselves but shadows of a shadow-world.

Saint Paul affirms that there is a natural body, and there is a spiritual body, and goes on to tell of his experience, how he "was caught up to the third heaven, and heard unspeakable words, which it is not possible to utter." We cannot dismiss the otherwise reliable witnesses by labeling them mystics, for truth must stand by itself and cannot be confused with personalities. The *Book of Revelation* contains nothing save the experience of Saint John when his spiritual vision was focused on the other world, and this book is accepted by all Christian churches. In the vision of hell, purgatory, and heaven, as described by Alighieri Dante, we have an encyclopedic view of highest culture and knowledge of his age, expressed in exquisite poetry with consummate power and beauty of language. John Milton, some time before the Restoration, rapidly composed *Paradise Lost*, not based on individual experience, but as an epical treatment of a sublime subject. It is said that Goethe labored for many years on his masterpiece, *Faust,* and that it was not completed until he gained a knowledge of spiritual world influences. Emanuel Swedenborg, a scientist of the eighteenth century, after studying and writing on scientific subjects for many years, experienced a vision of the spiritual world and has given a comprehensive account of the matter. As several of his valuable books on this subject are published by Everyman's Library, no doubt most persons are informed on his views. It is said of Swedenborg:

And thus prepared, all nature at his feet,
    At God's command, to higher realms he soared;
He mapped the heavens, the spirit world complete;
    Hell's lowest depths were ev'n by him explored.
With opened eyes and mind alert, he walked
    Throughout all regions of the other world;

With angels, aye, with devils too, he talked,
To give to earth the secrets thus unfurled.

Enough has been said and written on the subject of the spiritual world to show that human thought has at least an idea of the future world on which to build its hopes and conclusions. We may assume that the Kingdom of Heaven is not a fixed state; it has changes that are evolutionary, for its mental and emotional qualities are always in fluxion. It is composed of individuals who were first born into our world, where they acquired a training and experience which fits them for tasks far beyond physical endurance, and challenges their spiritual abilities. As these individuals pass over into the next world, with their new and personal abilities, their influence must continually alter the conditions and arrangements of that world. Physical death is actually a blessing in disguise, for it releases one from material limitations, and widens the horizon of our usefulness. No one, faced by death and eternity, no matter how talented or fortunate, ever claims that he has attained his highest purpose or completed his ambitions. There are always unfulfilled aspirations that demand a new set of conditions in which to find satisfaction. The education and training acquired in this world have no equivalent in gold, in property, or in positions of power. Our real values are accumulated in unconscious moments, in solitariness of mind and soul.

The spiritual assets of an individual are not visible to the world. They begin accumulating in childhood and the accretions continue through the years. In moments of unselfish devotion, the tenderness of pure affections, tolerance of others' opinions even when they affect our position, the mercy shown to the weak, the ignorant and the innocent, the solving of problems by exercising generosity, the craving for all that is

good and true, create a spiritual wealth which is not
corruptible, but is imperishable. Every person has
spiritual values which are seldom if ever used in this
world; they are secreted in his soul as the eternal
increment which serves as a passport to the next world.
These are the fruits of that love "which suffereth long,
and is kind; that envieth not; vaunteth not itself, is not
puffed up, doth not behave itself unseemly, seeketh not
her own, is not easily provoked, thinketh no evil;
rejoiceth not in iniquity, but rejoiceth in the truth;
beareth all things, believeth all things, hopeth all
things, endureth all things."

Few individuals recognize the established operations
of the mind because they are habitual, and therefore
never analyzed. These modes are accepted by a person
without question, yet in them are the qualities which
make for character and personality. Man is an embodiment of some type of love, and his affections operate
on the things of his interior memory. The emotional
thought then proceeds to ideas which are formed in
the external reason. These ideas then emerge in
words, deeds and gestures, which are heard and seen
in the material world. When any word is spoken, or
any action taken, it signifies the method by which affection is expressing itself. The affection and desire are
the inmost motivating germ, it is clothed first in
thought, then by ideas, and then comes forth as speech
or act. How this operates can be observed by noting
the tones of a man's voice, and watching the emotional
fiber of the voice; the use of words betrays the state
and quality of the affection. The personal affection
also animates and influences the blood of the body,
shows itself in the features, and reveals itself in the
eyes. The operation is successive and simultaneous,
and is an indication of the quality and genius of the

individual; it is the distinguishing mark of personality, and makes him unlike any other person. This order of expression is a fundamental principle of action, it is habitual with man because it is imposed on him by the forces of the spiritual world, which are preparing him for their kingdom. Fichte says:

> Love is life. Where I love I live.
> What I love, I live for that.

Because of this spiritual world dominance in human affairs, whatever experience a person has, even to the smallest particulars, has as its purpose the development of character; for the individual loves and affections are forced into action, and thus become fixed and habitual. This is the chief reason why man is placed in the material world, and tested by varying occurrences through experience. When the affection and desire mutually agree to serve others unselfishly, they are united to other affections of a similar kind; and from this arrangement associations ensue in which each derives its satisfactions, and the entire community is given the advantage and profit. When the desires are evil and for self-interest, they operate in the same manner, and by the reverse order the community suffers. From these studies it can be seen that every individual is in training for the Kingdom of Heaven, and yet he is permitted a constant freedom in expressing his affection according to his own methods, and even abusing them if he so elects. It is this abuse and neglect which unfit him for service in the other world, and his unsocial habits bind him to the under-world of compulsion.

Swedenborg said, "The very life of man is his love; and such as the love is, such is the life, and even so is the whole man."

To every man there openeth
A way, and ways, and a way,
And the high soul climbs the high way,
And the low soul gropes the low;
And in between on the misty flats,
The rest drift to and fro.
But to every man there openeth
A high way and a low;
And every man decideth
The way his soul shall go.

Man has two memories. He has an assimilative memory which is sensuously aware of worldly relations, and stores impressions that can be recalled at will. There is also a potential internal or spiritual memory. This dualism of mind permits the individual to make two general approaches to his problems. The external is the mechanistic or laboratory method. The internal makes its contact with spiritual things and retains the essence of thought and feeling. Knowledges are acquired by the external memory from things of the world outside itself; for there can be no thought without imagination, and the imagination deposits its impressions in the external memory. Men who do not reflect do not know how the habit of understanding, thinking, judging, and concluding, has been formed; but the result of those conclusions and apperceptions is indelibly impressed upon the internal memory, and their quality and volume are according to the genius and nature of the individual. Every man sees things in his own way, and forms his own opinions regardless of others. The internal memory, disposition, and genius are individual to man; and the faculty and capacity of the external memory have their origins in the native powers of the spiritual memory. Shakespeare, in the fifth act of *Richard III*, describes the play between the two memories:

> O coward conscience, how dost thou afflict me!
> The lights burn blue. It is now dead midnight.
> Cold fearful drops stand on my trembling flesh.
> What do I fear?
>   myself?
>   There's none else by:
> Richard loves Richard; that is, I am I.
> Is there a murderer here?
>   No.
>   Yes, I am;
> Then fly.
>   What, from myself?
>   Great reason why:
> Lest I revenge.
>   What, myself upon myself?
> Alack, I love myself. Wherefore? for any good
> That I myself have done unto myself?
> O, no! alas, I rather hate myself
> For hateful deeds committed by myself!
> I am a villain:
>   yet I lie, I am not.
> Fool, of thyself speak well:
>   fool, do not flatter.
> My conscience hath a thousand several tongues,
> And every tongue brings in a several tale,
> And every tale condemns me for a villain.
>
> There is no creature loves me;
> And if I die, no soul shall pity me:
> Nay, wherefore should they, since that I myself
> Find in myself no pity to myself?

There is something within man, the I am I, which is his dominating principle, it is in his constant thought, and he loves it above everything. It rules his actions and constitutes his essential self. In dreams, the internal memory excites the memory of material things, for the external retains his ideas of lineaments, motions, speech and gestures, and all material facts, and the dreams would be impossible, and a vision worthless, without the aid of the external faculty. The interior memory has the faculty of perception and intuition, which is exercised and developed when man has a kind disposition toward others, and when it is concerned with spiritual truths and internal reflection. The spiritual memory selects from the external those things only which it can use in its operations, it eliminates those which do not harmonize with its nature, and repudiates those which disturb its peace. Therefore much of our superficial knowledge is of no value in the formation of character. The operation is automatic and by unconscious complementation. We forget what does not interest us; just as the eye does not see all that it looks at, and the ear hears those sounds only that agree with its moods. We could not reason logically without the functioning of the internal memory, nor could we distinguish between truth and error. It is by exercise of the internal perception that we know a statement to be true, even without considering its arguments; and by the internal intuition we recognize instantly the degrees of love, and the nature of evil hatreds and subtle devices. When a person passes from this world into the Kingdom of Heaven the external memory sinks to the lowest level, its sediment acts as a buffer between the higher things and those beneath, but the internal memory remains, for it is the intellectual basis of the new life. Since the internal memory retains the essence of all of its reactions, nothing of the past is lost, it can recall the causes and relations of every experience, and connects them with its knowledge of the states through which it is to pass. It is this

understanding and comprehension of the universal relationships which unite each individual with the group in
the spiritual world of which he becomes a member.
The power of the group in the understanding of itself,
and of coördinating itself with the universal spiritual
world, produces realizations which are beyond words
to express. We cannot escape the truth that man is
bound by his essential nature to the purposes and
conditions of life.

From the observations made of the intellectual and
emotional nature of man we may safely conclude that
there is a keen sense of perception operative in those
who enter the Kingdom of Heaven. When one individual approaches another in the spiritual world, the
quality of the thoughts and affections is instantly perceived. These perceptions are a faithful guide, for not
only is the quality known at first contact, but the persuasions and types of argument; for his nature is apparent in each idea and gesture. The communication
is by means of ideas and the color given them by the
affections, and the interchange of ideas is easy and
pleasant, with its accompanying delights.

While man lives in the physical world it is possible
to experience a small measure of this perception, but
it is hindered by anxieties concerning the future, by
animal desires, by thoughts of food, of domestic duties,
and ambition for advancement to positions of power.
All of these encumbrances are removed, at death of the
body, from those who are charitable; and the perception becomes keenly active as gross bodily sensations
are discarded, and disturbing emotions dissipated. One
of the effective results of the faculty of perception is,
that it enables a society of the spiritual world to dis-
engage itself from that which disagrees, and to con-
join itself with those that harmonize; in this operation

each society is individualized and kept distinct. That which disagrees cannot disturb, for it cannot enter a contrary sphere, it cannot even approach or endure that which is opposite to its own nature. Individuals in the spiritual world are always in the order of their affection and function. The communication of the individual is with the inmost of his own group, and the communication of the group is with the most interior of the kingdom, and the government of the Kingdom of Heaven is from its center, and from thence to each least division and part. Thus is coördination established by means of perception, and the knowledge of the quality and service of each society.

Perception has its basis in the intellect and the affections, and when these agree, the quality of the harmony is imparted to the perception. Thus a man can perceive what he ought to do, and is inwardly persuaded, because the mind presents those things which are affirmatory, and in which there is little that contradicts. If a person thinks solely of his physical, he cannot enjoy the faculties of perception and persuasion, for the senses will not admit the truth of anything which they cannot feel or analyze. As an illustration let us consider the experience of one who reads a book; if he is intensely interested, his thought goes beyond the subject matter. As his senses are inactive he is elevated into a clearer perception of the subject. His thought does not dwell on the typed words, and he comprehends the matter without reading. Thought may often, when thus awakened, go off on a side line, the lungs do not dilate or contract, he is outside himself and realizes the ultimate object of his thought. This power of perception may give some idea of the functions of the spiritual world, and their contact with men who are in our world. In these moments details are recalled which eluded his former thought, the ideas are fitted together, and the connections completed. We may be assured that no exceptional invention, no outstanding musical composition, no illuminating idea, ever comes directly from the producer alone; the contact and illumination are from the spiritual world, and both sides share in the result.

There are times when the whole world mind is in a certain mood; it will accept innovations which would have been rejected at other periods. There are political moods, literary moods, industrial moods, and when they are operative everything is favorably accepted. These moods are not self-invented, nor are they artificially produced or controlled, for they have their origin in the spiritual world, in the concord established for the moment between the two realms. In the mass, men are said to be emotional rather than intelligent; this is true because inclination is stronger with man than aspiration. The higher faculties of perception and intuition are based on intellectual experience, and not on physical sensations; on the essence of things, and not on their material substances.

One of the accomplishments of the radio is that it has taught us the art of tuning in on the melody and eloquence of an otherwise closed world. And this should remind us that the creative process is perpetually active in the world, in things material, in things mental, and in things spiritual, and that we can observe its operations if we watch closely, and can hear its melodies and symphonies if we hold our ear to its vibrations. Sir James Barrie says there are times when "beauty boils over, and then spirits are abroad. Ages may pass as we look and listen, for time is annihilated." Astronomers can see new worlds in the making, and bacteriologists can watch germs in the ferment of evolution. In nature, beauty and rhythm have a still, small voice, and to one who is sensitive it makes him well-nigh hold his breath for its unfolding helps, in simple and real ways, to understand the more evident problems of existence. The Hebrew prophets begin their exhortation with the words, "I heard the voice of the Lord, saying," or "Thus saith the Lord." They stood on the mountain tops from whence did come their help. Wordsworth says:

One impulse from a vernal wood, may teach you more of man,
Of moral evil and of good than all the sages can.

We are on the border-line of worlds, and sensitive to nature's spell and guidance, and the transition from seen to unseen is simply a shifting of the mental eye. Theodora Thompson says, "There is in each of us, what Ruskin called a touch-faculty, by which we can have access to the vast, unguessed powers that are always, and everywhere near us. The difficulty is to realize, not only the range and extent of these powers, but the variety and beauty that are packed away within the reach of everyone and within the soul of everyone. We stand in the midst of a universe so immeasurably above this in splendor, in beauty, in variety, in the perfection and relation of all of its forms, that words cannot describe it." This faculty of seeing the unseen has been practiced by ancient races, and has been the mainstay of their faith. The Book of Job gives this advice, "Speak to the earth and it shall teach thee." It is from those men who have held communion with the invisible that we gather wisdom; they have looked into nature and read her secret, they discover some old truth and tell it in a new way.

Great is that man who stands so high
Two worlds are captured by his eye:

He sees these little days of Time
Whirled into a drama, vast, sublime.
Earth has a meaning fine and far
When lighted by a mystic star.

The song that has no sound has no appeal for the man who is walled in by the five senses—he considers beauty, art, and music as illusions. No doubt much has been lost in modern days by mechanized music, for the rhythms have become fixed; symmetry of phrase and regularity of cadence hold the structures rigid. We are confined to two simple rhythms, a rise and fall of two beats and a rise and fall of three. In the music of primitive people the emotion and feeling of the singer or player varies, and no song is ever the same, for the individual improvisation is active. Among these people, music is melody unfettered by harmony, free in pitch and rhythm, infinitely various and flexible, curving, rising and falling, soaring, fluttering, tracing the immaterial swell of emotion. We may rest assured that music has an important place in the Kingdom of Heaven, for music, color, and sound are three methods of expressing love and truth; and each group expresses its affection by characteristic melodies and corresponding colors. Men in our world could be affected by the spheres of the spiritual world if they were open to the influence. William Blake has often regretted this loss of beauty and values; he has said, "If the doors of perception were cleansed, everything would appear to man as it is, infinite. For man has closed himself up, till he sees all things through the narrow chinks of his cavern."

In the universal plan of life every individual must be permitted freedom in choosing what he likes, but having made the selection he must accept the consequences and abide by his personal decision. He is not hindered

in either the use or abuse of his knowledge, for he has
a native knowledge of that which is evil and that which
is good. It is granted that much of his sin and unsocial
act are due to ignorance, and to neglect. The neglect
of his finer faculties and their perceptions accounts for
his ignorance, but never having developed those higher
capacities in this world, they are useless to him in
the spiritual world. The pity, then, is not the sin, but
the indifference to the full call of life, the neglect of
opportunity, the ear closed to high adventure; and all
this in face of the fact that the whole universe constantly invites him to enter its secrets, and learn nature's story. Character is fixed in this world, because
all the incentives to learning are in its copy-book. When
we pass over, when the veil is parted,

> We are ourselves
> Our heaven and hell, the joy, the penalty,
> The yearning, the fruition. Earth is hell
> Or heaven, and yet not only earth; but still
> After the swift soul leaves the gates of death,
> The pain grows deeper and less mixed, the joy
> Purer and less alloyed, and we are damned, or
> Are blest, as we have lived.

Physical death does not remove individual characteristics, neither does a mental profession of faith
absolve the past, for in the Kingdom of Heaven it is
impossible to conceal the real man. The mental state
we carry over does not rise to new elevations; it expands and increases within its own boundaries. Only
that which a man actually has remains with him as his
own; he can find no new oil for his lamps once the gate
is closed. Knowledge of good and evil are acquired
through the experience of success and failure, and the
experience teaches one the means of safety. It is also

true that action at decisive moments calls forth unused energies and neglected talents. It is said that the chief obstacle to serious thought is stupidity and a congenital incapacity for thinking. Capacity for thinking is no assurance of other world success, but gentleness of disposition and charitable deeds are more in demand. Men learn the nature of good from practice, and not from mental cogitation.

The prophet Micah sensed the truth when he said, "What doth the Lord require of thee, but to act justly, to love mercy, and to walk humbly with thy God?" In the presence of truth and beauty, first we are surprised, then we admire, and this stimulates emulation. Thought is created and sustained by spiritual substances, and to one who can see when he looks, the natural forms of this world indicate their spiritual origins. Everyone has the capacity for understanding higher truths, because the inner light of his soul illuminates his natural thought, but he cannot be sustained on this elevation unless he fixes those truths in his acts and deeds. When his thought descends to the world, he denies the spiritual truth and calls it illusion or delusion. Therefore, justice, mercy and humility are the fixatives of truth. Truth is light, and when a silver-sensitive film is exposed to the light, it will not reveal the picture unless the film is developed and fixed. The acid bath for truth is in the chemical laboratory of daily duty and service. It requires a developed spiritual sight to comprehend the truth and beauty of the Kingdom of Heaven. An evil disposition not only darkens and perverts the light of truth, but it destroys the spiritual vision. The intellectual mind dallies amid the brilliance of truth and beauty, and like a moth before the light, it is paralyzed into inertness. The most ordinary of us know moments when we glimpse the concealed beauties of the spirit world. We may not have the words to describe them, and we are loath to speak of them, but to every one is given the opportunity to express them in sympathetic and portraying deeds.

All men and women know moments when a tumult of seldom experienced, and consequently more valued, impressions, created a sensation of unusual warmth around the heart. We all treasure the recollection of such moments and wish for their return. Shelley must have been in such an emotional condition when he produced *The Skylark*. Prolonged solitude helps in understanding our inner selves. The works of Charles Dickens live to-day because he walked the streets of London in the small hours of the night, accompanied only by the invisible characters born in his books. He could not separate himself from them until their lineaments were fixed on the pages of his manuscript. It is fortunate that each of us was a child at one time, and it is well for maturity to recall and react its childhood, for children under ten are poets and philosophers. A little boy who would not leave the seashore was chided for looking so long at the waves. His excuse was, "They watch what I am watching, but they do not see what I see." The observing child, like Berkeley, shares the philosopher's doubt concerning the existence of the physical world. A little girl who was playing with her doll while her father's friends were discussing reality put them to silence when she asked, "Father, what is beauty? What makes it?" This world is packed with miracles and wonders, but the secret doors are hidden unless one finds the way and employs the key. What did the poet Gray have in mind when he wrote:

Full many a gem of purest ray serene,
    The dark unfathom'd caves of ocean bear;
Full many a flower is born to blush unseen
    And waste its sweetness on the desert air.

The difference between learning and knowledge is one of adjustment and vision. The great author, Balzac, produced nothing but verbal trash between the ages of twenty and thirty, and then after an internal revolution he created masterpieces. The prophet Isaiah in his book indicates a heavy, disconnected literary style in the early chapters, until he came under the influence of a compelling impression of the glory of the Lord, and after that he expresses the beauty and elegance of diction. He traces the national corruption of the Hebrews to a single source, the absence of a spiritually religious consciousness. The decadence of Israel was wholly due to lost vision, and they survive only in their inspired prophets.

Truth and love are eternal substances, and every person is capable of reacting to this substance, and the character of the individual indicates the measure of his responses. Thought is formed from the observation of objects, learning the mode and rule of their action, because this observance excites the senses. The external pictures can be coördinated with man's thought for they have an order and sequence, and this order is the pattern of man's internal self.

Existence for man is not possible without sensation, and the degree of response is according to the sensation. The faculty of intelligence is an exquisite sense of interior truths, as is also the perception. There are sensations which are real, while others are imaginary. The origin of sensation is the individual affection; love is the mother of truth. The physical senses spring from desires and serve them; the touch-sense is the affection for good; the taste-sense is the affection for knowledge; the smell-sense is the affection for perceiving; the audient-sense is the affection for obedience; the sight-sense is the affection for intelligence and wisdom. It is remarkable that the clue to the internal meaning of the Scriptures is in the understanding of these principles, for the inspired writers of the Bible invariably clothe their inmost thought in common words drawn from the experience of the senses. All spiritual life revealed in the Bible is depicted in human experience. Every character has a relation to something within human thought and emotion.

The soul has sensation as well as the body; the spiritual senses penetrate the causes and principles of life; the physical senses react to material things, and are gross in comparison to the others. All of the senses have their origins in the affections which are the center and core of the man. Therefore nothing can be sensated unless the affections are aroused, for sensation is a method or technique, and not a substance in itself. A person has no interest where his affections are not concerned. Those who hate others and covet their possessions stoop to crime because their interest is in their own welfare. Those who love most, suffer most, because wrong-doing reacts upon their inmost love. Sensation absorbs some of the qualities of its own affection, and therefore there is desire in every pursuit of sensation. We may readily conclude that the several societies of the Kingdom of Heaven are intimately related to the human feelings of men on earth, and as these feelings change, the connection is made with the society that agrees with the sensation. When an individual passes to the next world his external senses do not function, and in their place he has the exercise of

those spiritual senses which were partly developed by
existence and training in our world.

> Between birth and death is the Road of Life
> each soul must travel alone;
> And to some that road is a pleasant one as
> o'er it they happily roam.
>
> Sometimes our road other roads will cross as
> onward we journey alone;
> And great is our joy when we meet a soul
> whose road is much like our own.
>
> For into the world you have been sent for a
> purpose known only to One;
> So, in faith and hope, and with courage firm,
> go onward until your journey is done.

The human family cannot be separated, for it is a
unit eternally. To arrive at any other conclusion would
be a violation of the order of life. When the ancient
theologians imagined heaven as the abode of the
blessed, and confined the evil individuals to the damna-
tion of hell, they regarded the separation as an act
of divine justice. But divine mercy takes care of the
unadjusted and unplaced; hell differs from heaven in
its functional operations, but both operations have
their uses. The human family has its external and its
internal, its non-coördinated and coördinated, just as
the physical universe has its chaos and cosmos. In the
lower levels of the spiritual world are the undeveloped,
the retarded, the inefficient, the unadjusted; they are
in the depths not because divine edict has condemned
them, for they have not developed their potential resources, and cannot make the grade. By habit and
practice they have alienated themselves, and the discontent produces the ferments and bacteria that infest

all forms of life. They know nothing of the felicity and order of heaven, for they have no feelings that register either of these conditions.

In the phenomena of the physical universe non-coördinated change is more violent than coördinated change, and out of the chaos of molecular collisions there comes a volume of cosmic energy. We may rest assured that the ferment of the lower world has its place in the orderly sequence of life. Coördination creates new energies, and the Kingdom of Heaven holds the human family in connection; not only those who are in our world, but all those in the other world.

It is not the aggregate number or the concourse of individuals that makes the Kingdom of Heaven the dominant power, but the functions and services that they perform. The unit is estimated on the performance of its abilities, functions, pursuits and occupations. The function is according to individual affection, and each love is different, but when they are brought together they form a perfect unit.

In the physical body, it is not the number of parts or organs that compose it, but the aggregate of functions, which makes it organic. No two cells are the same, and no two operations are alike. It is the united effort for the general welfare that combines and attracts them. This law is true in the Kingdom of Heaven; there are as many affections as there are uses, and there are an infinite variety and species of both. Affections are the continuations and derivations of love, and love has one goal in view, and that is to give full expression to life, and therefore all love returns as in a circle to the source of its origin.

There is a circle, or orbital movement, in all things, and this is its activity and energy. The movement begins at the center; this may be illustrated by a human act—sensation operates in a gyre as it proceeds to action. First, the internal sensory perceives and understands. It resolves the things understood into thought. From things thought it judges; from things judged, it selects that which agrees; and so it concludes, wishes, determines, and acts; and this action produces an effect that fulfils the end desired and understood. This rotation or circle operates as sensation goes through its changes to complete the action.

The process of purification and perfection is not accomplished by liberating the discordant and contrary, but by removing them from its circle. We can visualize the circle of life from our own experiences; by means of the senses the individual creates a memory; from the memory the mind elevates impressions into thought; the thoughts which harmonize with the individual affection constitute the substance of the will; and the will is the actual life of the man.

It will be recognized that the principle of the circle is universal in its applications and operations; it is in constant movement and agitation. When an individual passes over to the spiritual world, he speaks and acts from those things which he has experienced within himself, for his will is the substance of the individual. There is nothing sudden in the transition. The other world is not unusual, it is in accord with human expectation.

> As what he sees is, so have his thoughts been.
>   Whether he wakes
> Where the snowy mountains pass,
>   Echoing the screams of the eagles,
> Hems in its gorges the bed
>   Of the new-born, clear-flowing stream.

Whether he first sees light
  Where the river in gleaming rings
Sluggishly winds through the plain;
  Whether in sound of the swallowing sea—
As is the world on the banks,
  So is the mind of man.

Vainly does each as he glides
  Fable and dream
Of the lands which the river of Time
  Had left ere it woke on his breast,
Or shall reach when his eyes have been closed.
  Only the tract where he sails
He wots of; only the thoughts,
  Raised by the objects he passes, are his.

CHAPTER XI

THE KINGDOM COMPARED TO THE BODY

IN THE Kingdom of Heaven the direction of government does not reside in any one person, but rather in the highly developed center of each group or system. The organism of the Kingdom can be classified in systems, and these again subdivided into societies, very much like the organism of the human body. The government is devoted to strictly human needs, which are those of growth, development of function, and continuous life. Doctor MacIver, in a recent book, has said, "Life is that which feels and knows and wills, that for which values exist, and which itself exists as a value." In the Kingdom of Heaven there is a perfect coöperation of the individual societies with their own system, and of these larger combinations one with another. Each works to sustain the life of the whole. Since the ultimate goal is consciously entertained by all, each individual functions in an orderly way to maintain the united government.

The motive which holds each individual to his society is the love of being useful, and this one motive permeates the entire government, fixing the position of each society to its system, and then each of these to the complete unit of the Kingdom. The manifold abilities of groups, which ability and use are individual, are coördinated to the eternal good of all. We are requested to regard the human body as an illustration of this central principle, for in the body we discover the life to consist of the coöperating functions of cell, corpuscle, nerve and organs.

The layman will readily understand that the human body has its separate systems, each with its own particular duties, and that health depends on their coöperation. To classify these systems in a general way, let us name these divisions: First, that which gives rigidity to the body, the cartilage and bones. This can also include the skin and the hair, all of it built up by the lime salts called calcium. Second, the muscles, ligaments, and tendons, the semi-fluid fleshy parts of the body, which are flexible and wonderfully interwoven and compacted. Third, the arterial system, the capillaries, veins and heart, taking up the food-essences, and the oxygen, and conveying the material to all parts of the body. Fourth, the alimentary canal, embracing the mouth, stomach, and intestines, which convert the raw food into substances which the body can absorb and assimilate, and rejecting the coarse and unwholesome parts. Fifth, the respiratory organs, centered principally in the two lungs, where the valuable oxygen is taken in and the poisonous carbon dioxide is thrown off. Sixth, the glands, liver, pancreas, kidneys, spleen, the chemical laboratories of the body, where fine discrimination, separation, and manufacture of products are in process. Seventh, the nerve system, with centers in the brain, medulla oblongata, and spinal cord, where the complicated lines of communication bring in the sense impressions. Eighth, the generative organs, which respond to sex instincts, and operate to procreate offspring.

Every anatomist and physiologist knows how these organs are related according to function, that they are not grouped together but distributed in all parts of the body, and how they are subdivided into cells, composed of complicated molecules. The action of light from outside, and the continuous flow of fluids within, produces chemical reactions in the body with results which are electric, and these can be accurately measured. The energy by which the physiologic processes are sustained is the product of these reactions. It is a wonderfully inter-related organization.

Merely to describe the processes of the human body, limited as is our knowledge of them, would require many volumes. It would be wise to confine ourselves to the elementary facts and to simple statements, for our knowledge is always subject to revision due to constant changes and new discoveries. Our object is to summarize our knowledge and to apply it to an understanding of the processes active within the Kingdom of Heaven, where societies and systems operate in a similar yet more perfect accord.

We should not minimize the importance of the individual in the Kingdom of Heaven, for while the other world is a unit it is composed of individuals working in personal capacities. The personal consciousness of identity is never lost. In the human body the single cells are not conscious, although responsive to external stimuli, but they are exceedingly important, for each cell is in itself a chemical factory of secretions and excretions. These cells can change their relation to the work in hand, the bone-building cells reverse their actions, they often tear down what they have built. Molecules constantly regroup, as work demands, they do this regularly in the expansion and contraction of the muscles. The red corpuscles of the blood are continually changing their position in the blood stream; they load up with oxygen at the lungs and unload at some distant muscle, like honey-bees, that take on the syrup and pollen and deposit them in the hive, and then retrace their steps and begin again.

Some organs of the body sublet control. The brain, which commands the nerve centers, sublets control of the muscles to the spinal cord. The human mind can detach itself from the brain, delegating the operation, and thereby concentrate on things more abstract. The physical body is the most perfect mechanism in the world and the marvels of its operations tend to increase as we learn of them, rather than decrease. Vitamins are exceedingly useful in food digestion and health. They are so minute that chemists have difficulty isolating them, and their existence was unknown at the beginning of the year 1900. The smallest factors in the chemistry of the body are often the most important to life and health. It has been recently stated that calcium compounds introduced into the body produce a visible effect in the enamel of the teeth inside of one minute. In understanding the importance of the cells and of the minute chemical elements in bodily operations, we can learn how essential is individual and small group action in the larger government of the spiritual world. The preponderance of effect is not to the mass, but to the individual.

Men, for many thousands of years, have been living in physical bodies and have been aware in a general way of their operations, yet it is surprising that even to-day we have no complete knowledge of their specific functions. In the same way, man knows very little of civil government, or of its orderly laws and principles. Much that is called scientific remains theoretical and speculative. This may explain why fads of all kinds become popular, why there are so many doctors and so few physicians, why some medical rooms are crowded with the latest mechanical apparatus as a pretense of knowledge, and why so many human guinea-pigs are subjected to experimentation.

Normal relations between organisms involve a large amount of biologic reciprocity. Obligations and duties devolve on all, and to sustain their life they must contribute to the welfare of the organic family. This requires effort, ability and coöperation in creating and utilizing natural riches. This truth applies equally well to the human body, to civil government, and to the Kingdom of Heaven. We shall discover, before our study is completed, that these three organisms are closely related. The totality of organisms, whether in plants, or in the human body, are a type of world-society; and, just as in human societies, the success and the progress of the individuals depend upon the character of their mutual relations and behavior. There is a right action and a wrong action in things animate and inanimate.

Just what it is in the human body that gives each group its capacity of function is the problem of the biologist. How they do work is now intelligible to science. But, why they do so, and why they coöperate to achieve one particular end, is not known. This phase of the subject is beyond the realm of matter and the laboratory, it belongs to the province of the mind. Psyche means mind, and the further pursuit will carry us to the psychic realm, and it is here that the fuller knowledge of the organism of the spiritual world can assist us.

Francis Darwin has recently said, "Evolution now becomes definable as a process for drilling organisms into habits, and eliminating those which cannot learn." It is known to scientists that there is a "civilizing" force in nature, due to the labor and coördination of all of its parts, and it is said by some that a sort of moral conscience can be attributed to nature, which affects sex, structure, status, and biologic correlations. We know for instance that the individuals of society have ability, and that these abilities and talents vary to such a degree that no two are exactly alike. Socrates is recorded as saying, "I consider that we are born not perfectly resembling one another, but differing in disposition, one being fitted for doing one thing, and another for doing another thing." The non-vitalist will say that the acid and temperature condition of our bodies induces the varying moods and dispositions, and that pain and pleasure are due to states of the nervous system. This is a part truth, but not all of the truth. Nerves, acids and temperatures have something to do with moods and dispositions, but the potential mood and disposition exist prior to, and are inherent in, the nature of man as man.

Coöperation of cells in the body, and of men in society, does have some repressive force. Some possible function is given up because it can be better performed by some other person or group, but a salient talent and ability remain for the individual energy. The Mendelian theory explains how our abilities may be compound and complex forms of cross-inherited tendencies and urges, but it does not explain why man has ability and why life would be a failure without it. Chromosomes act chemically and mechanically, and they seem to act with purpose, but native ability is not a chemical or mechanical attribute. No doubt each individual has several abilities *in potentia*, and while his situations and opportunities are developing one native talent, the others remain in the background. We have seen how cells of the body can reverse their operations. A master musician might have developed his ability in the art of the brush or the chisel, as artist or sculptor, for these abilities are related. But he would be a failure as a mechanic or tradesman. Abilities are innate and inherent and not acquired. This truth is illustrated in the concept of the Kingdom of Heaven, where every individual finds his exact place according to the nature of his ability to perform service for the whole unit. There is nothing to prevent him from going at any time to some other group, or from changing his work. This possibility of change is granted. The same principle of change is demonstrated in the human body, where cells move about and are allocated to the immediate need. In the study of individual characteristics we may gain some knowledge of behavior from chemical life of plants. Prof. J. B. Farmer, in *Plant Life*, writes, "In the evolution of the more complex plants, the cells—the primitive individuals—become organized into a higher individuality," and he shows, "that the nucleus, the true determinator of hereditary qualities, is the seat of individuality." It is when we transcend the narrow confines of physical, chemical and physiologic divisions that we get a comprehensive view of the matter without injustice being done to any associated factor.

The author of *Nutrition and Evolution* says, "The normal relations between organisms, more particularly those having regard to food, involve quite independently a stupendous amount of systematic biologic reciprocity, so that upon all organisms there devolve definite duties and obligations, on pain of degeneration and destruction, to contribute in their several ways to the welfare of the organic family as a whole." The human body develops its growth from food, and there is a wrong and right use of the incoming material. When we lift our thought to the processes of the Kingdom we find that there are societies organized in a system of inspection, separation, and education, which take care of the incoming material. The supply coming into the Kingdom of Heaven originates in the world. It consists of those who pass through death to the future life. There is a constant stream passing from this world to the next, and it is estimated that some three thousand pass over during every hour of the day. The good in their affections, and the truth in their knowledge, separated from evil and error and retained. The fallacies, unsocial habits, and abnormal desires are stripped off and rejected. Each individual is educated and trained so that he may become a working member of the great organization, and he moves to the sphere and society for which his qualities best fit him. The coördination of these individual activities is the fundamental fact of life, not only in the Kingdom of Heaven, but in all the phenomena of nature from the plant and vegetable kingdom to the organic life of the human body, and should hold in the organized social government.

In the spiritual world each society and group has its peculiar and individual work; there is a coöperation of all conditions favorable to a high degree of reciprocity from every part of the complex organization in which the polity of the whole governs. There is nothing unusual, startling, or novel in it; the individual recognizes his place in the scheme of things. The mechanical and chemical energies are dismissed, or rather translated into a higher type of activity. The reciprocal action of love and truth, their reactions one upon the other, are now dominant. Love and truth are actual substances and realities in the new life. Imagination, ideas and impressions, and thought, are transparent processes and open to instant inspection. It is not a nebulous world, for there are objective phenomena corresponding perfectly to the things thought, loved and spoken. The truth and the love, as expressed and felt by the individual and the society, create the external scenery and situation.

When the mechanics of this world are removed, the pace becomes a thousand times more rapid than anything known by us here. Volumes are expressed in a word, in the inflection of an eyelash, in a smile. There are no ambiguity, no misunderstanding, no misconception; the nature of a thing is accurately and instantly known. There is more leisure and perfect peace, for there is no energy lost in friction, everything is simple and there is no possibility of the make-believe. Orderly procedure eliminates false motion and misdirected energy. There are no mental illusions or abnormal desires to combat. Some one will say that this is picturing the ideal, but is it not humanly possible? Every mind at some time idealizes such a future state. There is an effort here and now to attain it on earth. Every person is in the endeavor of creating for himself just such a condition. We have the effort in embryo, in many forms, and therefore what is to prevent eventually the realization of so human an idea? Human nature furnishes us with all of the ingredients, elements, and qualities; the true reason is that we have never separated, assorted and rearranged our own human qualities in an orderly manner so as to achieve our goal.

As a people we have never had the courage or ability to coördinate and adjust our best human potentialities. We have misused our possessions and talents, and never directed them unselfishly to the welfare of all mankind. What group or nation has ever been actuated by the disinterested desire to do right, regardless of consequences? How many really want to live serviceably, in the pursuit of good and truth for its own sake?

Let us suppose for a moment some form of government in this world where equity and justice would prevail; where money would be discarded, and there would be a free exchange of products, and where life in its fullness would be the goal; where talents would be grouped, each group contributing its best to the common welfare, and where the mutual desire would be to develop the higher human attainments. The necessities of food, clothing and shelter would be supplied by the groups having this particular occupation in charge. Other groups in exchange would supply these groups with their needs.

In such a social order how would the medical profession fare, for we can take it as an example to illustrate the process. The talent and ability of the medical profession would be classified and arranged in order so that the problem of physical health could be adequately met and solved with the least waste of effort. The sole attention of the surgeons, physicians, and specialists would be centered on the one task, for all of their material wants would be supplied by other groups. This would include the necessary equipment, apparatus and chemicals, so that the profession would have no anxieties as to food, education, or instruments. Naturally the system would divide into smaller groups, located in chosen centers. Each group would have its specialists, bacteriologists, pharmacologists, and psychiatrists, the central control board making the proper selections and transferring the workers as needs developed.

The governing board would consist of the recognized men and women of executive ability, unhampered by politics. With the profession devoted to the one supreme end of community health, preventive measures would be studied, and the so-called incurable diseases would command expert attention. Adjustments to the problem, and corrective measures of dealing with stubborn forms of disease, would suggest themselves as the task developed. Every member of the community would have confidence in the preservers of health, and every one would be free to consult them, and the profession would welcome the public participation. Communication of ideas, and a common interest in all new discoveries, would prevail. There would be no pampering of the rich who are under the delusion of imaginary ills, for in this government there would be no idle rich.

There would be schools for the education of young men and women; the quacks and mountebanks would be eliminated. There would be openings for all grades and types of ability. In the field of education there would be contacts with the clergy, the scientists, the social workers, and the legal fraternity, with a full and free exchange of information and ideas, and an explanation of the technique of the medical aids. This coöperation would suggest itself within the common needs, and it would concern sanitation, eugenics, wholesome foods, housing, athletics, sex control, and childbearing. The entire problem of health would be attacked by efficient and scientific methods and the results would be revolutionary. The problem would be pushed back from cure to prevention, and cases would be treated in their first stages.

Can anyone fail to recognize the results which would follow this aggressive mass attack on disease and ill-health? Nor would there be any doubt as to the pleasure which the profession would experience in its great work. The morale of the body politic would be amazingly changed. Fear would give way to confidence, for the disease-bound energies would be released, and a great burden would be taken from the shoulders of society. The daily loss and waste of disease would be turned into valuable channels and into common assets. This experiment in government is certainly worth trying, and would mark the turning point in civilization and culture. We have taken the medical profession as an illustration, and by applying the same principle to all professions and labors, the ideal government is seen as a reality here and now. It is a world possibility which can be eventually realized.

If biology were not prejudiced in favor of purely mechanical interpretations, it could throw more light on social and economic problems. The fault is not in the available facts, but in the weak interpretations. It may be said by the biologist that economics, or the science of wealth, has little to commend itself, for there is no parallel to it in nature, except as a disease breeder. Herbert Spencer has said, "A grave responsibility rests on biologists in respect of the general question, since wrong answers lead to wrong beliefs, about social affairs and to disastrous social actions." It may also be said that the pioneers of evolution have misused the theory, and evolution has been dubbed "the dismal science." But Francis Darwin has recently expressed a better thought when he says, "Evolution now becomes definable as a process for drilling organisms into habits, and eliminating those which cannot learn." This view fits into the proper conception of life. In regard to the main goal of life, the poetic Ruskin has written this, "A truly valuable thing is that which leads to life with its whole strength, in proportion as it does not lead to life, or as its strength is broken, it is less valuable; in proportion as it leads away from life, it is invaluable and malignant."

In any study of sociology and world government we

must not neglect the basic facts of life, for each succeeding realm, from the lowest upward, furnishes its
illustrations and lessons. The Greek mind was pos-
sessed with the idea of a world in leasts and a world
in greatest. It is worth noting that it was a physician,
Alcmæon, who first formulated the concept of the
macrocosm and the microcosm. In the ancient schools
of medicine the heart and lungs were regarded as the
main centers of life. To-day we know that life depends
upon the coöperative labors of a complex organism in
which every part performs its service and from which
it receives its rewards. It is in these coöperative partnerships that life has its solutions.

There are many myths of the dead brought back to
life. The incident of Empedocles and Pantheia shows
how they were attributed to the genius and skill of
famed healers. Wherever we choose to place the seat
of life, there is an unmistakable analogy between the
human body and the forms of political government.
If the governing centers of a man's body are working
properly, we may expect health and life, but once disease and disorder are at the core there is small hope
for continued existence. If a toe or finger is cut, a bone
fractured, a ligament torn, or the scalp injured, a general alarm is sent to the brain and mind, and the healing balm is sent to the rescue, provided the central
powers are sound and active. But, once the disease is
at the center, in the heart, the medullary centers of
the brain, or in the secretive glands, any permanent
cure is impossible.

In a civil government, whether by king or parlia-
ment, or in a Republic of executive, legislative and
judiciary, if a rebellion or disorder of major proportions occurs in the provinces, the difficulty is brought
under control by the central powers. The same would

be true in business, transportation, or agriculture. But, when the heart of a government becomes corrupt and abnormally unbalanced, then the existence of that form of government is approaching the end. Every death of an individual, of an institution, and of a nation, can be cited as an illustration of this truth. It is in the history of Egypt and Persia, of Russia, and of Spain.

The life is continued only as the coöperative activities function. Division of labor means that every part has to undertake a particular kind of work, the specific work requires individual ability and produces healthy reactions. The more thoroughly the work is done, the more completely does the special reaction predominate, and the more developed is the ability. Go into whatever realm we choose, and it will be demonstrated that man cannot be divorced from all that exists below him in nature. Man in his destiny is inseparably linked to them by the eternal law of organic sociology, and his origin and future must be understood in the light of that relation. There is a civilizing force in nature and its laws, and it is here that man first learns his lessons.

> Heaven is not mounted to on wings of dreams,
> Nor doth the unthankful happiness of youth
> Aim thitherward, but floats from bloom to bloom,
> With earth's warm patch of sunshine well content:
> 'Tis sorrow builds the shining ladder up,
> Whose golden rounds are our calamities,
> Whereupon our firm feet planting, nearer God
> The spirit climbs, and hath its eyes unsealed.

Until social government is revolutionized so that the fundamental urges of man's spirit can be satisfied with normal outlets, the conflict of human interests and the sufferings and penalties of misconceptions will inevitably result. Man has only recently acquired a knowledge of his physical structure, he knows little of his mental faculties and processes, and he has shown limited desire to apprehend the indisputable evidences of the superworld. When he begins to understand himself and his relation psychologically to the social world around him, and to the spiritual world within him, there will come the dawn of a new government of men. No one, no matter how great the insight, can measure the invisible stature of man's undeveloped spirit.

The common run of men may appear bewildered and mentally immature, and socially maladjusted. The viewpoint depends upon the kind of light we have on the picture; there are regions of dark pigment, but the final effect is with the highlights. There are thinking men who do emphasize life-situations and the lessons of experience, rather than naked materials. There is progress from the realm of matter to the possibilities inherent in spirit. The difficulty is in combining the intensely evident and the abstractly possible, to unify technique and theory. The student of social science hesitates to enter the arena of public politics and the urgency of immediate affairs, because he knows there is no formula of hasty results, and no panacea for human ills which can furnish quick relief. Evolution is patiently slow in its processes and operation. The student of economics and politics, of religion and education, and of ethics, feels that the unmeasured ignorance of the masses is the retarding factor in any attempt at progress. He cannot identify himself with the moods and uncontrolled emotions of the human family.

It is possible that the accepted reasoning is not on a secure basis of facts, and that a new method must be devised in dealing with the subject. The same statement has been made until it is believed, and it may be necessary to revise the belief that people desire solely their own interests and not that of society, and that the lack of information makes them easily the victims of the frothing demagogue and the self-elected pleader. It is claimed that men have no taste for statistics, that they cannot discriminate between fact and opinion and are incapable of sustained thinking, and that government cannot be understood unless the mathematical rules of Euclid are applied to its solution. Let it be said in answer to this that the individual human mind is limited in its capacity to entertain many thoughts, and that only by the combination of a variety of minds can any problem be solved. Each individual and group has its allotted function, and when these are coördinated and made active, the aggregate is equal to any task. Great thoughts and ideas remain a heritage to mankind, they may be dormant but they cannot die; out of this accumulated increment, under the pressure of immediate needs, man must finally build his world society.

The forces to be dealt with are complex; one set does advance at the expense of others, and there is always a decided disproportion, but that does not mean that they are beyond the power of coördination and established order. Humanity can become oriented to its actual world if it combines its abilities and forces. It is quite evident that the issue of a final solution in government cannot be forced, but it can be wisely guided and apparent obstacles removed, so that the human family can discover its own best interests as of one household. There are events and circumstances rapidly shaping themselves in the world which are creating an atmosphere and encouraging the latent and retarded desires into stimulated action for liberalization of the human talents. The value of control is recognized in the desire and exercise of this liberty. Daniel Webster in his Charleston speech expounded the principle when he said, "Liberty exists in proportion to wholesome restraint."

All are aware that we are in a changing world, which implies that the world can be adjusted and brought into systematic order. There is an observed wave line in the progress of evolution, in which the advance meets with a reverse, but the point at which it rests is always higher than it ever stood before. Evolution does not run in circles; while no issue is settled for all time, when it does recur, the new generation can, if wisely guided, readjust the traditional to its own necessities. When the importance and possibilities of the inner world are understood, human energies can be joined with the higher power, and the conquest of the material values achieved. The human race is bound by invisible ties with the Kingdom of Heaven which cannot be dissolved, and the reconstruction of society depends upon how faithfully the spiritually evolved pattern is copied. The persistent effort to attain orderly consequences in human affairs has its origin in the concealed, impelling urges emanating in that world. The human desire for order is not in itself selfish, nor are we fully conscious of its ultimate purposes, but it is so insistent that it cannot be eternally defeated.

In the world's social evolution, students may discern the emerging cartilaginous form which outlines faintly the new order possible to the world. The discoveries of science have produced a new body of facts which can be summarized philosophically, and the material in hand is sufficient for correct conclusions. The former interpretations have been hastily stated. Largely materialistic, they are not in agreement with established truths. There is a recognized relation between science and the other departments of learning. We are now aware of an international mind, an inter-relationship which includes all of the human family. Each nation may be thinking in local terms, but its modern interests go beyond territorial borders, and each contributes to world needs. The master minds of every race are exchanging and sharing ideas and thoughts, and thus creating a common brotherhood. The repercussions of an acute situation in any nation are felt in the governmental centers of all peoples. Human nature is beginning to secure control of its own fluctuations, and this in turn encourages an affirmative state of mind. It is an acknowledged principle of spirit that the finer illuminations can come only into the affirmative mind, into its faiths and beliefs, for these are the forms capable of receiving spiritual light.

Progress is not in conflict, not in unsocial acts, but in challenging questions by the serious application to solutions. Man has potential abilities which can create his social structure, and their orderly definition will be expressed in patterns that fit his constructive needs. There are civil and moral laws, the observance of which lead the way to spiritual and social freedom. Individual behavior operates on three planes, material, mental and spiritual, and when consistently expressed it will insure humanitarian welfare.

A society in which the saint and the apostate, the good and the evil, the honest and the criminal, the educated and the ignorant, exist side by side may be difficult of control, but our physical bodies which discard the poisons and adjust all of the elements to a useful end furnish a pattern of centralized government which it would be advisable to emulate socially. When we grant the proposition that everything in the universe can serve the use of man, we must admit that evil and ignorance can be commanded in the service of social good. Proceeding on that principle, the control of these human factors, not only present in the individuals of the group, but in each one of us individually, is in relegating them to the level on which they can serve the good of the organization. They are the forms of ferment and bacteria, important in the equilibrium of government only when confined to their respective places and functions. It is a universal fact that man fears evil and its consequences, and until he learns how to conquer and use it, he cannot be expected to evolve an orderly government. Fear is an unnatural obsession which retards the facing and solving of the issues of life. Government cannot arise from chaos until every human factor, by adjustment and coördination, assumes its orderly place in the social fabric. Human beings are easily influenced through their passions and prejudices, and there is a law which, when discovered, will equally influence and stimulate the finer and nobler qualities.

There is a known pattern of government in the physical body. There are clearly defined groups of activities which are inter-related and act in conjunction for the health and well-being of the body. There are elusive chemical and electrical forces in the body the functions of which are not yet understood, but the general structure of the organism has been analyzed sufficiently to assist with its lessons in the art of social reconstruction. It may be argued that a chemical organism cannot be expected to furnish information for the conduct and control of human beings in government.

In the discussion of this proposition there are several arguments which have a bearing on the problem. Everything in the known universe has an orderly procedure; it obeys an unalterable law. There is a definite principle which governs all activity, regardless of the particular field or department to which it is confined, and this governing principle is never violated except at the penalty of non-activity or death. Whether in any given field, chemical, electric, humanly emotional, mental or spiritual, the principle is the same. Every expression of life has its relation to the order of life; the form of the original is stamped on the product.

Another fact which must be held in consideration is that the human element enters into the chemical direction of the physical body, and that the intention of the body is to adequately express, in visible act and vocal word, the affections and thoughts of the human being which inhabits it. The activities of the body are not entirely mechanical or chemical, nor should they be defined solely in terms of service, for there is an atmosphere of spirit and of human will which cannot be dismissed or excluded from consideration. Just as the single body becomes a vehicle of expression for the individual, the social system is capable of being molded into a form which will make articulate the spirit of the group and the nation.

In the social systems of law and government there are mechanical operations, but these are not the vital concerns of life. The composite sphere of human emotions and thought is the propelling force of society, and the educational and legislative machinery is the channel of expediency for the communication of human thought and the radiation of human desires. In all sociologic calculations the truth must be recognized that there is a world within the world, composed of urgent motives which spring from the emotion and thought centers, and in which love and hate, self-sacrifice and covetousness, sex-passion and the love of home, persistence and indolence, and desire for peace and harmony, play their part. It is this explosive inner world which gives luminosity and color to all the activities of society. There are mystics who affirm that our supposedly repressed emotions, given no outlet, are absorbed by the furniture and fabrics of the dwelling which we inhabit, and held in bondage there concealed, they have an effect and influence on those who enter the room. Not disputing the theory, we must admit that the spirit of man cannot be divorced from the machinery of his social order, or the visible work and creations of his own hand.

If there is any just and satisfactory form of government to prevail in the world, it must spring from the educated and awakened consciousness of man. It will be in the rational response to the insistent inner demand, and in the willingness to lend oneself to the task. The type of government will then be patterned on an orderly and consistent plan, and be in line and conformity with the normal human rhythms. Sufficient has been disclosed to prove that the government of the physical body offers such a plan. Its working parts are easily classified into definable systems. Each system is distinguished by its particular function, and the combined uses are coördinated as an organism of effective service and purpose.

In the social world the talents, abilities and capacities of the people are various, but the variety lends itself to a universal harmony because related to the one purpose of expressing life in orderly consequences. The major task of social organization would be in defining and classifying the abilities so that they could function intelligently and with a definite goal in view. In the physical body the function performed by any system is not localized, the active individual cells of a given system are separate as to space, but united as to function. The individual must perform his uses at the point of its need, regardless of its location.

When viewed in this aspect, a parallel can be observed between social government and the physical body. The firm basis of social government is the home and family, and its relation is seen in the bones of the physical body. The bones not only support the weight of the body, but they protect its more delicate and sensitive parts. The bones enlarge in proportion as the body develops, in the bone-marrow originate the new cells of the body, and in the teeth the bones perform a careful supervision over all things which enter into the body. The salient place of the home in government, and the family ties in developing the young, are of fundamental service to the state. The reader can pursue this line of parallel reasoning and discover for himself the close affinity of the body of man with his external world.

The alimentary canal and digestive system suggest immediately the preparation and processing of foods, which embraces the agricultural interests of men, the cultivation of the soil, the manufacture of implements, and the culture and fertilization of growing things. There is a vast amount of talent called into action in the production of food. The aptitudes of many persons turn involuntarily to the pleasurable contacts with the soil, to mother earth. They enjoy planting seeds, in seeing things grow, and in gathering the fruit of the field. If left free to follow their own desires they would overcome the criticism of Shakespeare when he said that "we are creatures that look before and after, the more surprising that we do not look around a little and see what is passing under our eyes." If this gift of seeing and feeling were unhampered by problems of finance, something for which these minds are not fitted, and unlimited by vexing questions outside their particular province, the art of agriculture and the harvesting of fruits and grain would provide an untold measure of satisfaction, and its product would be for the nourishment of the nations.

Respiration is a wholly dissimilar system, it deals with the more rarefied and gaseous elements, it fixes in concrete and useful forms the substances of air and breath, and conveys them from the lungs into the blood cells. It suggests the processes which make thought concrete, the abstract is made practical, and brought into fixed and measurable objects. This is the function of the educational institutions and vocations. Here we have the ability of scholars, teachers, writers, lecturers, musical composers and dramatists, and all that the word education implies, as a necessary function in civilized communities. To organize this ability and give it a field of operation where it can work for the good of the entire social world, and to free it of those destructive incumbrances which afflict society, would be an achievement of first importance.

The muscles of the body give it pliability, they hold parts together, keep the bones in conjunction, control the blood and food movements, and release the sensations. This system corresponds to that of civil relations in matters of business, trade, exchange, and all of the operations and duties which must be kept fluid and maintain the orderliness of association. It includes the higher type of diplomacy which defends us from recessions into the pathologic world of abnormal psychologies. The muscles are fed by the products of the lungs, the compounds of oxygen, and in like manner the civil relations subsist on right and logical thinking and intelligent action.

The skins and limbic coverings prevent overlapping and establish order in the realm of individual functions. They conserve energy and the surfaces segregate resources and keep them in reach of the active forces of the cells. This implies a function which remains largely undeveloped in any social government. Political borders are now defended by armies and navies, a policy which is contrary to social welfare, inconsistent with any theory of social harmony and destructive of international relations. When social governments are founded on the principle of the conservation and protection of functions, rather than on preserving racial and national frontiers, military defenses will disappear, having outlived their political necessities.

The office of the heart in maintaining the blood stream, with its capillary fields reaching to the remote parts of the body, and working in conjunction with the lungs in purging the body of its impurities, is manifestly an important means of service. Perhaps the ancients were not far in the wrong when they assigned to the heart all of the emotions called love. Since no government could exist in perfection unless good-will, brotherly relations, and the warmth of sympathies were maintained, there must be a system corresponding in some way with this function of the heart. There must be provided something which will provide vitality and preserve the purity and harmony of human associations and relations. Regarding the failure of the world of to-day and of yesterday, what could have been more essential to its well-being than the exercise of those deep feelings which religionists, mystics and romanticists call love? How this volatile quality could ever be controlled and become a department of government would be difficult to capture and assign; per-

haps it would be the accumulated product of every system, just as the blood stream is the common property of all of the body. There is a stream of current life which carries all before it, and which none can escape, and in it we all participate. Who knows whether it cannot be amicably capitalized?

The brain centers and the connecting nerve lines, keeping the mind informed on every changing state of the body, suggest methods of rapid and ceaseless communication. We perceive immediately the need of telephone, telegraph, postal-service, radio and aviation, as vital functions in regulated government. The terminal centers are in the groups which control each system, they decide from moment to moment the urgency of all important calls and relay their messages to those localities that await the advice. Coördination of the entire government is thus maintained and every situation is immediately met and order preserved.

The secreting and excreting glands are segregated chemical factories, yet having one main purpose in view, and that is to provide the exact material which any part of the organism may demand. The manufacture of those articles which are needful for human existence, supplied by factories, workshops and laboratories, that stimulate commerce, transportation and trade, while not particularly a part of government, and yet necessary adjuncts to human modes and customs, may be compared to these functions of the glands.

It may be said in objection that the plan proposed is too sketchy and superficial, that it fails to include many of the essential duties of government, such as legal questions, property rights, and the disposition of finances. Such a criticism has logic and force, but it may be said in rebuttal that any detailed and complete plan of social government which revolutionizes the present

system has not yet been born in the mind of any human being. All that may be legitimately expected is the presentation of new ideas, and the introduction of new facts, and that is the only contribution which this book claims to give. The perfect social government will never develop as the product of one individual; it is a problem the solution of which will require the accumulated wisdom of all thinking men and women, and in that mind finally rests the hope of the world. When it comes it will be realized in some unanticipated form, for it is always the new and unexpected which develops.

CHAPTER XII

THE KINGDOM OF HEAVEN INEVITABLE

I like the man who faces what he must
    With step triumphant and a heart of cheer;
Who fights the daily battle without fear,
    Sees his hopes fail, yet keeps unfaltering trust
That God is God; that somehow true and just
    His plans work out for mortals; not a tear
Is shed, when fortune, which the world holds dear
    Falls from his grasp; better live with a crust
Than living in dishonor; envies not,
    Nor loses faith in man, but does his best,
Nor even murmurs at his humble lot;
    But with a smile and words of hope gives zest
To every toiler. He alone is great
    Who by a life heroic conquers fate.

WE CANNOT survey the possibilities of the Kingdom of Heaven without taking into consideration the moral and mental state of the men and women living in our world, for they are the material from which the spiritual world builds its structure. The actual state and condition of the human element are not known to us; there is so much of man that is hidden from public view that no accurate survey of facts can be made, and therefore no reliable data are at hand. Every individual has spiritual potentialities which environment and opportunity never develop.

Man is the sum
And complement of every form in one
And universal, therefore, rightly tends

To uses manifold and like himself.
The greater part of man hath never yet
Flashed into action. But a narrow rim
Of his huge orb yet shines to light the world.

There are differences in personality—in emotional, volitional, affective and attitudinal traits—which are enormously influenced by the inherent and hereditary nature of the individual within his accidental environment. If the environment were absolutely identical there would still be unaccountable variations in intellectual and professional achievements. Every man has a vital and unknown asset in the genes within the sperm and ovum which form the unborn components of intellect, skill and character, which may and may not grant him the will to succeed in his undertakings. Therefore the behavior of individuals cannot be standardized, for there is so much of it that will fit into no category. The transgressions from normal rectitude, and deviation from established human and divine rules of conduct, are more than moral questions, and cannot be hastily judged by dogmatic theologic tribunals.

The attitude of Jesus is worth studying. He dined openly with publicans and sinners, he defended the adulterous woman, he invited the hospitality of Zaccheus, he knew that the woman who made him an object of worship was immoral, and Mary of Magdala was the first person to greet him after the resurrection. No one would sanely pretend that immorality and sin are orderly and unobjectionable, but that does not alter the observable facts of human behavior. Why do individuals seek escape from their better selves? Why does plain responsibility hang so heavily on some persons that they prefer temporary oblivion? In George Musgrave's version of *Dante's Inferno*, we read:

> Scarce had he ended ere the whole dark plain
>   Trembled and rumbled with such dreadful sound,
> E'en now cold drops of sweat bathe me again
>   At the mere thought of it. From underground
> The Land of Lamentation then unbound
>   A rush of mighty whirlwinds terrible,
> With the red flare of lightnings flashed around.
>   Whereat, losing all sense, beneath the spell
> Of overpowering sleep down I unconscious fell.

Can it be that the demands of life are so exacting, so exhaustive, so insistent, in finding modes of expression that the hesitant mind and physical frame are often shattered by the vibrations? The psychoneurotic often turns for relief to any intoxicant or narcotic that will afford delight to the senses and quiet, even momentarily, his mental functions. Every nationality has its favorite drug; every person seeks his recreation and rest from duty and conflict. Abraham Lincoln claimed that the nation which had no slave or drunkard would be highly fortunate. Broaden the connotation of slave and drunkard, the slave to some habit or form, the intoxicated by some zeal or cause, and who could honestly say, "In me is no sin"?

It is said that human vices have no counterpart in the behavior of animals, proving that human degeneration has been acquired at some stage of the social existence; but we do know that small insects at times lose their normal instincts for companionship and wander off in isolation to die alone. Deposits of bones, the remains of wild birds, are found in the Salton Sea, and game-wardens have seen tens of thousands of wild ducks plunging into waters seemingly seeking extinction. These facts prove nothing, for we do not know the actual causes for such behavior. But we do know that human self-interest can be attributed to social conditions over which the individual has no control. People seek self-preservation because they have lost faith in governments, for the government does not provide for its aged citizens, nor does it assure its youth of employment. The conditions imposed by many governments encourage individuals to protest against its regulations. When the true history of modern social and political revolutions is written it will be discovered that governments have failed because the ideals of youth have been shattered and lost. The backbone and stamina of a nation are in its youth, and when youth has been deluded by the conduct of its elders, the decay of that nation invites revolution.

"Youth is not a time of life—it is a state of mind. It is not a matter of ripe cheeks, red lips and supple knees; it is a temper of the will, a quality of the imagination, a vigor of the emotions; it is a freshness of the deep springs of life. Youth means a temperamental predominance of courage over timidity, of the appetite of adventure over love of ease. No one grows old by merely living a number of years; people grow old only by deserting their ideals. We are all as young as our faith, as old as our doubts; as young as our self-confidence, as old as our fears; as young as our hopes, as old as our despairs. There is latent in every being's heart the love of wonder, the sweet amazement at the stars and the starlike things and thoughts, the undaunted challenge of events, the unfailing child-like appetite for what next, and the joy and game of life. In the center of our minds and heart there is a wireless station; so long as it receives messages of beauty, hope, cheer, courage, grandeur and power from earth, from men and from the infinite, just so long are we young."

There are psychologists who claim that many writ-

ers attempt to escape from themselves and their neu-
rosis by producing endless manuscripts. The cause of
unsocial and selfish action lies deeper in the human
will than its surface indications betray. There is also
the other side of the picture which reveals those who
are determined to master their situations; Sara Teas-
dale has caught this idea when she says:

> I would not have a God come in,
> To shield me suddenly from sin,
> And set my house of life to rights.
> Nor angels with bright burning wings
> Ordering my earthly thoughts and things.
> Rather my own frail guttering lights
> Windblown and nearly beaten out,
> Rather the terror of the nights
> And a lone sick groping after doubt.
> Rather be lost than let my soul
> Step vaguely from my own control—
> Of my own spirit let me be
> In sole, though feeble mastery.

An individual, as well as a people, can never succeed unless aware of what is being done. Since the
Kingdom of Heaven knows its objective, and in that
knowledge selects each individual for the position in
its structure which he can fill with credit, the diversity
of talent, the amount of human achievement, the undeveloped faculties, are all adjusted so that there is
no disorder, no chaos in its government. There is in
every person a deposit of good, an undeveloped re-
source, which has retreated in the presence of external
evil, and thus secretly preserved. This residue is
brought to the surface after death, its activity subdues
the external nature, pushes it aside as of no immediate
interest, and qualifies the person to act in conformity
with his heavenly society. This residue of good is not

actually the property of the individual, but it can be made so by performance of useful service. Jesus recognizes the good in man, not the evil which is the result of compulsion. He said, "I come that they might have life, and have it in abundance."

The dominating and inmost idea of every person is the continuation of personal existence, for he fears extinction; the will to live and to express personality is so persistent that it carries him into the next world. The internal good makes it possible for even an evil person to be in the presence of the lower angels. All angels were at one time citizens of our world, and they sympathize with the efforts of those who come to them.

> Angels are men of a superior kind;
>   Angels are men in lighter habit clad,
> High o'er celestial mountains winged in flight;
>   And men are angels loaded for an hour,
> Who wade this miry vale, and climb, with pain
>   And slippery step, the bottom of the steep.

When the individual comes into the spiritual world he awakens under the care of angels of the higher order, who give him all of the service possible, and make him aware of the best within himself; their aura creates in him the desire to do his best so that he may retain life. As he gradually comes to himself, the higher angels seem to withdraw, but the separation is due to the state of the individual, and as the changes take place he finally comes into the presence of those who are of a kindred mind with himself. The person is somewhat surprised to learn that his body is real, it has all the powers of sensation, and those about him are substantial and real people. His body retains its resemblance because the external things of his mind are carried over and these form a filament or skin, and are the points of contact with others. None of the chemical or electrical elements of the physical body are preserved, but the functions which animated them in this world are still active in his spiritual body.

The mental and emotional states of an individual are in constant movement. There is a stream of changing states which can be observed by any person from experience. We have our blue days and off-days, and also the days of elation and smooth sailing. There is an ebb and flow of the tides, nature has her seasons, and everything which is receptive of stimuli responds in ways that cause constant alternations. This continuous agitation of the mind and emotions is within a circle, for each person has an orbit which his mind travels. The individual thus establishes an habitual state peculiar to himself, it gives flavor to his affections and color to his thought; its influence is so powerful that it is impressed on the functions of his body, often shines through his features, and, in fact, becomes an image of the man. It is a factor in determining health and sickness.

The habitual mental and affectional state creates an aura which proceeds beyond the limits of the body, and can be felt by others who are sensitive to its impingements. This individual aura is so firmly fixed that it persists after death, and in the spiritual world is perceived as an odor by the spiritual sensories. Separations and conjunctions are effected in the other world according to the nature of the odor; when offensive to others, they withdraw, and conjunction follows when they are agreeable. Each society therefore establishes an aura harmonious to itself, and the society is recognized by the nature and odor of the aura. The aura, or affectional and mental atmospheres of the societies,

proceed beyond their immediate presence and act on
the mental states of men and women on this earth.
There are certain times when the mood of a people
will accept any innovation and radical change of the
social and intellectual order, and other times when
these suggestions are resented. Public opinion, or the
will of the people, is an expression of the activity of
aura states. As Lowell has said:

> For nothing comes between
> The senses and the spirit,
> The Seen and the Unseen.

Whatever a man loves most, that he fears to lose.
Often at the hour of death it becomes evident what
the person has loved, and what goal he has had in
view. Solomon has said, "Keep thy heart with all dili-
gence; for out of it are the issues of life." If the delights have been in material things, the person fears
death, and his thought will be upon those things around
which his interests are centered. This fear is dissipated
by the angels who are drawn to those who pass over
to the spiritual world; the love of material things is
subdued, for contact with them is gradually severed,
and the individual is reduced to the activities of his
internal nature. Errors of reason are corrected, and
fallacies of the senses are discarded. This separation
of the internal nature from the external is similar to
disrobing, and the outside garments of the mind are
laid aside. The individual comes into his own affection
and thought, freed from incumbrances, and nothing
that is valuable in personality and character is ever
lost. Those who have maintained the love of beauty
and truth throughout their earthly career feel this
release with a fine sense of joy.

There are in this loud, stunning tide
  Of human care and crime,
With whom the melodies abide
  Of the everlasting chime;
Who carry music in their heart,
Through dusky lane and wrangling mart;
Plying their daily task with busier feet,
Because their secret souls a holy strain repeat.

Thus everyone recognizes himself as he really is, the principles which belong to his nature stand out, and all that disagrees is forced to the outer fringe and lies there inert. This process of revealing the actual man, not only to himself but to others, is necessary so that he may be segregated and find his place in the spiritual society where he can be perfected and function. On this side of the veil his relatives and friends mourn him as one who is dead, while on the spiritual side he is welcomed as one newly born into the activities of their realm. Therefore the passing from one world to the other is not painful to the mind, there is no sense of time in the operation, and no feeling of fear at the final moment of passing, for the aura of the highest angels pervades and guides every transition.

When the individual awakens to the sensations of the other world, he gradually regains consciousness, and finds himself in the presence of those who have preceded him. They render all manner of service, supply all his wants, and answer all questions. The delightfulness of his situation has various reactions; those who are interiorly good confess themselves unworthy of so great rewards; those who are evil recoil from the attentions, they are bewildered and confused as by an anesthetic, and fall into a stupor that drops them to lower states. Conversations in the spiritual world are not carried on by use of words, but are a communication of thoughts and ideas, and as every person is more or less skilled in the art of thinking, the ideas are instantly recognized. What a man has thought in his solitariness while in this world becomes habitual with him, and it is often this meditation and thought that reveal the nature of the individual. Ideas and convictions which have never been expressed here become common property over there. It may thus be seen that man does not need to learn a new language, for the wisdom and goodness of a person are instantly expressed in his eyes, face, and slight movements of his lips. His beauty of features is according to the fullness of his ideas and their harmony with truth. By this method, more can be expressed by a movement of the eye or tremor of the lip than can be told in a volume of words. While on this earth an individual turns his spiritual thoughts into natural ideas, but in the other world that transformation is not necessary, for the arrangement of his thought has in view the ultimate welfare of his society.

In our world, man practices the art of reflection because he loves himself above all things. If he did not reflect he would know nothing of his physical sensations. He even reflects upon the activities of his own mind, and compares his thoughts and moods, and adopts a method of acting so that he may impress others. If he is studious and seeks to learn the truth, he can understand his interior motives, and can control their action. The sources of truth are all around him in our world, and if he examines the history of past experience, observes the wisdom inherited from the ages, and keeps abreast of the valuable discoveries of modern science, he will come into a state of thought which has everlasting values. This wisdom will be retained after death if he has controlled his behavior, disciplined his animal nature, and thus built enduring character.

We may accept as conclusive, Goethe's aphorism expressed in *Alles Vergängliche ist nur ein Gleichniss*:

> All that doth pass away is but the form
> Reflected from the real that remains.
> 'Tis I that bear within me peace and storm,
> The world with all its losses and its gains.
> Even the body's shape and all its sense
> Is but the mirror wherein I may scan
> My inner self,—but bear the mirror hence,
> Or break to atoms, still remains the man.
> So death may change the outer circumstance
> But to reveal the real world within,
> And let me see, in one astonished glance,
> The vision of my virtue or my sin;
> And going forth from out this shattered shell
> I carry with me my own heaven or hell.

The Hebrew prophet Hosea has said, "Come, let us return unto the Lord: for he hath torn, and he will heal us; he hath smitten and he will bind us up. After two days will he revive us: in the third day he will raise us up, and we shall live in his sight." The idea conveyed by all literature which attempts to describe the other world is that we leave this present conflict and arrive at a state of peace. The truth is that while we do change the substance of our bodies, we do not change the quality of our minds. The serious thinker who has been trying to act justly in human affairs is developing motives which can never forsake him, for he has vision, he sees where others do not. He has not acted in obedience to recipes, he has endured ferments, and the mental effervescence has clarified his character. His eyes have not been focused on realities but have gone straight to essentials. A person does not acquire wisdom from the images held in his memory, but from consideration of those things that concern his loves and desires. He makes an inventory of his loves, he separates the evil from the good, and dismisses those that degrade him, and by this method creates a nature which ultimately enjoys the delights of heaven. If there were no organized Kingdom of Heaven, man could never come into his own, for he would be an unfinished product.

The Kingdom of Heaven establishes an order which is reflected in the entire universe, it keeps all varieties and species in the line of evolution, it has its influence on the education and progress in human thought; its effects are less noticeable in human affairs, for man, unlike creations below him, exercises a freedom of action which often disturbs the order. But the order cannot be defeated even by man, for at death every man is regimented to the spiritual order.

> Earth is an atom floating in the light
>   Of summer sunshine with its kindred stars;
> A dewdrop shaken from God's blossomed thought.
>   He suffers evil in it for an end;
> This end is, like Himself, divinely good,
>   And pure and sweet, and infinitely free
> From pain.

Men have always felt the challenge of their environment, and their occupations have been developed in an effort to adjust the things of the world to human convenience and comfort. They are primarily forced to this action by the necessity for existence, for they must earn their bread by the sweat of their brow. When a higher state of intelligence is reached by a people, the menial tasks are given to the uneducated, and the superior minds reach out into the unknown for larger discoveries. This awakening brings a new meaning to service, for the conviction is born that individuals cannot succeed unless the level of the group accomplishment is also raised. A new ideal takes root in the community mind, the conscientious person is honest in business dealings, respects the home of others, is helpful in civic affairs, and responsive to the finer appeals of culture. The new idea of service is indirectly from the forces of the spiritual world impressed on the receptive minds of men, and furnishes an explanation of the sacrificial performance and service which animates those men who have an honored place in the estimation of mankind. It is the spiritual incentive which makes men aim high in hope and work, because they are creating structures that will elevate future generations. All men are at some moments religious, but some men are always religious in their devotion, love and loyalty, to those fulfillments which they consider imperative in the upward progress to eternity. It is true that man is born an animal in a mechanical world, but in his best moments his aspirations survey timeless and eternal things. For them, existence attains rationality only as it succeeds in turning animal instincts and physical energies to ideal uses and spiritual fulfillments. It is therefore that in this natural world we come in contact with the basis of our ideals, for they are real only when they can be tested here and now. If they stand up under that test, then the ultimate perfection is an achievement for the superior world. This world is the testing tube of character, but close to the conflict of earthly things hangs the invisible spirit of another world watching over her own and assuring success. Longfellow knew the power of spiritual substance which the eye cannot see:

The spirit world around this world of sense
  Floats like an atmosphere; and everywhere
Wafts through these earthly mists and vapors dense
  A vital breath of more ethereal air.

It is therefore true that in the spiritual world the occupations and professions are those of spiritual service not dealing with matter. The internal motives are directed to those uses which concern the welfare of others, and are in harmony with the new environment. The ends and purposes which became habitual with them while on earth imposed a character on the individual, and it is this character which expresses itself in new and superior ways. Within the universal communication of ideas, their native qualities discover realizations because of the attainment of new strength of understanding. In that world they do not act from instinct, but from intuition and perception of the real meaning and purpose of life. They discern and describe the inward purposes of art, science, and religion, in new modes, which were only dreams here, expressing them according to their native aspirations and intentions. In our world they turned nature to human account, and in the other world they transform experience into luminous and vivid order.

As the Kingdom of Heaven grows in power by the addition of incoming talents from the world, there is a continual development of new functions, new and refined forms of creative service are discovered. How spiritual enlightenment brings this to pass may be illustrated from the facts observable in our world. The marvelous progress of industry during the past fifty years, and the consequent movement for better economic coöperation between nations, are the natural and normal concomitants of the scientific discoveries and their technical adjustment to human needs. They have been brought about by the wider thought and broader spirit, the keener sympathy and understanding in the complicated fields of economics, psychology, and morals. Even though there is a temporary breakdown due to the abuse of new power, the trend is unmistakable and points to higher achievement when the social order is adjusted. Out of the effort we have many new industries, trades and professions, which were unknown to our fathers, and all people have shared in the new discoveries.

Whatever the mistakes and failures of this scientific age, no matter how political governments have crumbled under the new order, regardless of the universal feeling of injured justice, and the economic hardships endured, let us not forget that the times are in the travail of child-birth, and that something new and unexpected will eventually make its appearance. The gestation process is not new, for by this same means every new age has come into the world, and it comes because the powers of the Kingdom of Heaven brood over the minds of men. In the last analysis the Kingdom of Heaven is inevitable and inescapable, for all consequences point to a final coördination of human energies, and the ultimation of life's purposes.

> Yet Love will dream and Faith will trust,
>   Since He who knows our need is just,
> That somehow, somewhere, meet we must.
>   Alas for him who never sees
> The stars that shine through cypress trees!
>   Who, hopeless, lays his dead away,
> Nor looks to see the breaking day
>   Across the mournful marbles play!
> Who hath not learned, in hours of faith,
>   The truth to flesh and sense unknown,
> That Life is ever lord of death,
>   And Love can never lose its own.

INDEX OF SUBJECTS AND REFERENCES